CAROLINA TRENDSETTERS

*Insights and Innovations from
Local Business Owners, Professionals
& Community Leaders*

Copyright © 2017 NMG Publishing

All rights reserved. No portion of this book may be reproduced mechanically, electronically or by any other means without the expressed written permission of the publisher, except as provided by the United States of America copyright law.

Published by NMG Publishing, Charlotte, North Carolina.

The authors and publisher have strived to be as accurate and complete as possible in the creation of this book.

This book is not intended for use as a source of legal, accounting, or financial advice. The information in this book is intended to provide basic information on the topics covered and is not intended to be comprehensive by any means. All readers are advised to seek legal and financial advice from competent professionals when making decisions related to investments, risk management, or any other topics covered in this book. The authors and publisher are not responsible or liable for any damages or negative consequences to any person reading or following the information in this book.

While all attempts have been made to verify information provided in this publication, the authors and publisher assume no responsibility for errors, omissions or contrary interpretation of the subject matter herein. Any perceived slights of specific persons or organizations are unintentional.

Any trademarks mentioned in this book are listed for reference purposes only and are the property of the respective trademark owners.

Table of Contents

Introduction 1
Rod Potter: Building Your Network with LinkedIn 5
Ken Lacy: Helping Our Military Veterans and Veteran Families on the Path to Affordable, Stable Housing 21
Curtis Hughes: Digital Transformation for Established Companies 39
Torie Mathis: Helping Entrepreneurs Develop Successful Businesses 53
David Angel: Risk Protection for Your Business and Family 71
Jim Zuelsdorf: Financial Planning for Business Owners and Professionals 89
Dominique Rice: Finding the Perfect Nanny 103
Robert Aliota: Building a World Class Industrial Sealing Products Distribution Business 117
Steve Olp: Helping Small and Midsize Businesses Succeed Through Technology 133

Introduction

The Charlotte metro area spans both North and South Carolina in the central Carolina piedmont region. One of the fastest growing areas in the United States over recent decades, the region is a major hub for industry, banking and other financial services, transportation, distribution, and sports at the professional and collegiate level. Growth has been fueled by a great climate for business as well as a great place to live, work, and start new businesses.

The professionals, business owners, and community leaders selected to contribute to this book represent a range of professions and industries in the region and are trendsetters in their individual fields.

Rod Potter is well known as a connector and networking facilitator in the greater Charlotte area. He is the founder and leader of over two dozen online and offline networking groups. Rod provides an overview of the benefits of using the LinkedIn platform to build a professional network.

After a distinguished military career encompassing both active and reserve duty, Ken Lacy founded and is leading Veterans Path Up, an organization based in Charlotte, but expanding across the United States. Ken describes the challenges facing many enlisted military veterans and how his organization is helping veterans and veteran families on their path to affordable and stable housing.

Curtis Hughes co-founded an IT consulting company that helped hundreds of businesses with employee engagement, customer relationship management, and big data projects. He recently joined an international company as CIO where he is applying the experience he has gained over twenty years of consulting to develop and implement new technology strategies. Curtis describes how established companies are making successful digital transformations.

Torie Mathis began her career in the military serving overseas, but an accident while serving led her to explore different avenues for her work life. She turned to advertising and marketing and eventually formed her own agency. Torie works with all types of businesses, but she really enjoys working with entrepreneurs who are in the early stages of business development. Drawing on her own experiences, she has expanded her services into coaching entrepreneurs to develop successful businesses.

After a successful career in college and professional basketball, and then transportation and TV station management, David Angel followed his father into the insurance business with Nationwide. He expanded his agency over the years with offices in both North and South Carolina providing risk protection services for business owners and professionals and their families.

Introduction

David describes the most important considerations for business owners and professionals when it comes to managing risk.

Jim Zuelsdorf was a small business owner of retail stores before devoting his career to helping people prepare for retirement. For over three decades he has been helping people acquire, grow and protect their wealth. Jim provides an overview of financial planning for business owners and professionals who often are so focused on their businesses that they haven't thought about developing a financial plan for retirement.

While enjoying her work as a nanny for different families Dominique Rice networked with others in the industry and learned that there is a frequent disconnect between families and their nannies. She decided to find a way to find a perfect mutual fit so she formed Perfect Fit Placement, a nanny agency. She has expanded the business to not only connect families with the perfect nanny, but also to provide short-term childcare for employees of businesses that partner with her agency.

Robert Aliota realized that he was meant to be an entrepreneur after working for a few years in the computer networking industry. After studying a number of opportunities he realized that industrial companies needed a better solution for engineered sealing components for use in their products as well as for process equipment maintenance. He founded Carolina Seal, now a leader in distribution of engineered sealing products.

After thirty years management experience in a variety of industries, Steve Olp acquired TEAM Technology, which provides a variety of IT solutions for small to large businesses. He has been growing the business organically and through additional acquisitions to support a larger group of clients. Steve describes challenges for businesses in managing their information and provides some keys to successful project management.

The publisher is donating all retail royalties on sales of this book to Veterans Path Up, an organization that helps military veterans and veteran families get on a path to affordable and stable housing.

Building Your Network with LinkedIn
By Rod Potter

Introduction

Rod Potter is known as a super connector in the Charlotte, North Carolina area. He is the founder and leader of 26 online and offline networking groups in the area. Rod is also a video creator, helping businesses increase their exposure with video marketing. He has been studying LinkedIn for nine years and is teaching others how to use this powerful networking platform to make connections, develop leads, build business opportunities, find employees, and find a job.

In this chapter Rod Potter provides an overview of the benefits of using LinkedIn and how to get started building a network with LinkedIn.

My First Networking Group Initiatives

About nine years ago I decided that I wanted to get more involved in networking with other business people in the Charlotte area so I started checking out a number of local networking groups and see what was available.

Although I saw some benefits of being involved, I wasn't so interested in the group formats I was typically seeing. At that point I decided to create a group myself that I thought would attract like-minded business owners and professionals. I went ahead and created a group, but soon found it difficult to connect with enough people that were interested in attending. In fact, I was getting such low attendance it became uncomfortable, similar to having a birthday party and nobody showing up. I knew that if I couldn't get this turned around soon, I would have to abandon the idea. I knew that my time was quickly running out and that I had to make some drastic changes if I was going to turn things around.

My first thought was to use Facebook to connect with other people. I hadn't really been using Facebook, but after looking into it, Facebook seemed that it was best used for keeping in touch with friends and family and not so useful for making business connections. At that point a friend of mine suggested that I look into LinkedIn because it was a connection tool for professionals and business people. I started learning how to use LinkedIn and rapidly learned that it is a powerful way to connect with a large number of professional business people, the same ones that I was looking to attract to my group networking events.

Once I learned how to use LinkedIn, it became my preferred platform to connect with other professionals and business owners in the Charlotte area. Before I knew it, I was starting to draw larger turnouts to my networking group events. As I continued to learn all of the best practices of using LinkedIn, over time I established additional networking groups in the area. People saw my successes using LinkedIn to attract large numbers and started asking for help using LinkedIn themselves. This grew into helping professionals and businesses grow their network through LinkedIn. To make life easier for my clients and myself, I developed an online LinkedIn training course.

Benefits of Using LinkedIn

LinkedIn is like a search engine for businesses, with over 467 million users as of early 2017. It's one of the best resources to find and interact with your target audience, whether you're interested in increasing leads and sales, building a professional network, looking for employees, looking for a job, finding business partners, and much more. LinkedIn is also a great way to stay in touch with clients, get more exposure, monitor your competition, and can also be used as a sale funnel. It's a great way to build your brand and to position yourself as the go-to expert in your industry.

At least 90% of all companies are using LinkedIn to find and recruit employees, so if you're looking for a job, LinkedIn is a place you need to be hanging out. LinkedIn also has customer relationship management built in so it's a good place to continue dialog with existing customers. If you're looking for a person in a specific position at a target company you can use the power of LinkedIn's search engine to locate that person. Since many profiles indicate personal interests you can have a head start in building a relationship because you will be able to find out what's important to them by looking at their profile.

It's my opinion that it's not worth doing something part way if you expect results and using LinkedIn is no different. To get the most out of LinkedIn, it's necessary to spend a little time getting to know how to use it as well as setting up your profile so you will be perceived as someone that others will see a value in making a connection with. After developing a good profile, making connections are critical to building your network. The balance of this chapter will cover how to organize your profile, make connections, and start using LinkedIn for growing your network.

Building a Professional LinkedIn Profile

A professional looking and complete LinkedIn profile is the foundation of your whole experience on LinkedIn. With today's digital attention span deficit society, initial judgments are made in a few seconds, so it's critical to put your best foot forward. It may not be fair, but the truth is that you're going to be judged quickly on the look and the content in your LinkedIn profile. If it's a fairly blank page without much substance and a viewer doesn't see an immediate benefit of connecting with you, you'll have a difficult time making connections, impressing a potential employer or a business prospect. Although it does take a little bit of time to create a good profile, it seems like a substantial percentage of

LinkedIn users just don't recognize the advantages of creating a professional profile. Even if you are not using LinkedIn directly to grow your business, people that are considering doing business with you are very likely to see your LinkedIn profile. One of the typical things they will do is an online search for you to see what they find. LinkedIn has a high level of authority among the search engines like Google, Bing, and Yahoo, so when someone is searching for your name online, your LinkedIn profile will generally appear in the top 3 results when someone "Googles" your name. That's another good reason to put together a great profile.

Your profile picture is important in creating the first impression. I see too many people cropping out their spouse from a vacation photo and then there's an arm around their shoulder in the picture. The best results are obtained with a picture from a professional photo shoot, but even a good headshot taken with a phone will work. An optional and often overlooked feature is the background cover image that goes across the top of a profile page. A good background image is a powerful way to attract attention and can include a brief headline on the benefits of connecting or doing business with you. You can also include a logo and a short call-to-action right there in the background image. Think of the cover image as the cover of a book. Without an appealing cover, books generally will not be picked up at a bookstore or purchased. It's important to follow the LinkedIn guidelines on creating your background cover mage to make sure that it will display properly when people are viewing your profile.

You have space right below your picture for a headline. The most common mistake I see is that most people generally just put their job title in the headline. This is the place to put a succinct benefit that you or your business provides to your clients. As an example if you are a marketing consultant that generates leads for small businesses, instead of the headline, "Marketing Consultant," you might want to use something like, "Marketing Consultant | Helping Small Businesses Attract More Customers With Lead Generation." Now instead of just being one of the tens of thousands of marketing consultants, you are identifying a very specific and attractive benefit for business that work with you. Once you have their attention, they are more likely to read more. Right underneath your headline, LinkedIn automatically displays some information generated from further down in your profile, such as employer or business, a school you attended, your location and your number of LinkedIn contacts. I'll talk about making connections on LinkedIn later, but be aware that the number of connections you have that LinkedIn displays is another factor you will be judged on when someone is looking at your profile. A very small number of connections does not match with the perception of someone influential. Note that once you have at least 500 connections, LinkedIn only shows 500+ on your profile page.

If you have captured a reader's attention, the key message in your summary statement below the headline has a lot more chance to be read. This is the place to summarize who you are, what you do, and how you help others. It's important to focus on benefits that you provide, whether you're a business owner, professional, or are interested in finding a new job. Most LinkedIn users just use this space as a resume, but this is where you want to make it about the benefits and results that you provide to the people you are trying to attract. As an example, for the lead generation marketing consultant this would be the place to provide example results businesses have achieved in working with you, who you help, and a summary of how you achieve the results. This is also where you want to include a call-to-action and some contact information. You want to make it easy to do business with you so include contact information such as a website url, email address, and phone number. Always make sure to include keywords in your summary related to topics your best prospects might be searching for. For our marketing consultant, appropriate keywords might include "lead generation," "customer attraction," "small business," "more patients," and so on. That way when someone is searching for one of these topics on LinkedIn your profile is more likely to show up.

The next area to complete is the experience and education profile. This is more like a typical resume where you list the colleges or schools you have attended and the various organizations you have worked for with job titles and a brief summary for each position. Just like best practices for resumes, include results you have achieved in your various positions. The space for your current position can include additional information on benefits of working with you that didn't fit in the space allowed in the summary. Again it is recommended to repeat or add additional calls-to-action and current contact information. The comment about keywords applies here as well. There are many optional sections available to include skills, specific accomplishments, publications, who you are following, as well as to show your endorsements, and recommendations. It doesn't take very long to put together your profile and don't worry if it's not perfect because it's really a living document and it can be updated and expanded easily at any time. Many people find that by going through the exercise they fine-tune and optimize their message to the very people they are trying to attract.

Growing Your Network of Connections

After setting up a good profile, it's time to start building your network by adding connections. It doesn't make sense to start building your network before you organize your profile because when you try to make connections with people they are most likely going to look at your profile before agreeing to connect. If you have a poor profile they may not connect with you and then you may have just missed the boat with that person.

To get the most out of LinkedIn, the more first level connections you have the better, so this is an important area to focus on next. LinkedIn allows free messaging to all of your first connections and you will be able to see all of their updates and posts, allowing you to be able to know them better. If you're choosing your connections properly these could be your prospects and existing customers, so it's another way to find out what's important to them and build better relationships. The other import point is that your first connections will see all of your posts, so if you publish an article on LinkedIn that discusses solutions to common problems of your connections, you can brand yourself as the expert on the topic. Like people travel in like circles and another advantage of having a lot of first connections is that you see all of their first connections, so another potential source of possible customers. You'll also be able to request an introduction to the first connections of your first connections, another way to explode your network.

The more first connections you have naturally increases your search ranking on LinkedIn. Recommendations and endorsements can only be provided by first connections, so another reason to increase your connections.

A perceived obstacle to building a large network is that LinkedIn strongly suggests that their users only connect with people they know. Since most of us only know about 50 to 100 people really well, it will be difficult for most to achieve a large network if following that suggestion. You can't build your network if you're only connecting with people you already know. You might as well just use e-mail because you've probably already have the email addresses of the people you know. I guess there is a motivation on the part of LinkedIn to limit the size of their users' networks so they can sell premium services to facilitate communication to a wider group of LinkedIn users. Anyway, I recommend developing a wide and large network and I personally have tens of thousands of connections on LinkedIn.

Your immediate goal should be to get at least 500 first level connections so your profile will show 500+ connections at the top, indicating that you have a big network. You don't necessarily have to spend a lot of time building connections. I've found that if you can just devote a couple of minutes per day, you can rapidly grow your connections. Clearly the more people in your network, the more opportunities there are to find people who may want to do business with you.

Endorsements and Recommendations

Endorsements and Recommendations show up within your LinkedIn profile but you generally need to be proactive and request Endorsements and Recommendations from people that are familiar with your work. LinkedIn Endorsements are like votes for skills that are listed on your profile. Connections that are familiar with your work may go to your profile and provide one or more Endorsements. More often you will need to request Endorsements from connections that know your work. I've also seen connections that don't know someone very well provide an Endorsement, maybe trying to attract attention or with an expectation to return the favor.

Recommendations take a few minutes and require that one of your connections specifically write a few sentences about their experience with you. Generally you're going to have to request recommendations from people that know your work and have had a good experience by working with you. In fact, LinkedIn even has a form you can use to request a Recommendation.

Endorsements and particularly Recommendations are a great form of social proof and after setting up a good profile are the next most important factor on your profile. Before deciding to work with a professional or a business, people will likely be comparing you to others. Having a nice set of recommendations will help set you apart from the competitors or at least help you match up with your competitors if they have good Recommendations on LinkedIn. If you don't have Recommendation showing on your profile the message being sent is that either no one apparently likes or does business with you. Prospects are more likely to gravitate to that other person that has some good Recommendations.

Using LinkedIn Groups to Build Your Network

LinkedIn Groups are a great way to increase your network and build relationships in the place your target customer base is hanging out. Groups on LinkedIn are based on a common interest among the members. As an example one of my groups, "Charlotte Business Owners," is focused on networking opportunities for business owners and professionals in the Charlotte area. Some groups are focused on fairly narrow topics like marketing for chiropractors. If you were trying to connect with chiropractors, becoming a member of such a group would be an excellent way to network with them. Some groups limit the amount of members or exclude members that are potential vendors to the key professionals in the group, so you will need to check the membership policies. Also most groups don't allow directly pitching the members with group posts. A principle to follow is to add value by providing insight, information, or suggestions that may be of interest to group members. A benefit of joining groups is that you can directly message people in the group, even if they are not first connections. LinkedIn changes policies over time on how many such members you can directly message, but this is a very good tool especially when the group includes people you are interested in connecting with.

One of the most powerful ways to use LinkedIn Groups is to create your own group around a topic that will be of interest to an industry or a professional group you are interested in building relationships with. As a group founder and leader you can set the group policies and position yourself as a subject matter expert. Your role as the leader should be based on providing value to the members and demonstrating expertise that will be useful to the members.

Ongoing Exposure

LinkedIn provides plenty of opportunities to get more exposure to your network. Writing and posting articles that may be of interest to your audience is one way to increase your exposure and at the same time build your brand as an expert. Your posts will be shown to your first connections and will also show up on your profile. Other actions like comments on your connections' posts also show up to your connections as well as when one of your connections comments on one of your posts.

This chapter has been a fairly brief summary of the benefits of using LinkedIn as a networking platform and how to get started using LinkedIn to build your network, connect with business leads and customers, find employees, find a job, and achieve other business and professional goals. I've been a student of LinkedIn over several years and have developed an online course that goes a lot deeper into using LinkedIn with a lot more information than is possible in this chapter. Information about my online course, "World Class LinkedIn," can be seen at http://www.WorldClassLinkedIn.com.

About Rod Potter

Rod Potter earned a Bachelors Applied Arts degree in Communications from Central Michigan University. He is best known in the Charlotte, North Carolina area as a super connector and master networker, having founded and leading a number of local networking groups.

Rod is a LinkedIn trainer, helping business owners and professionals build their networks, generate leads, build their brands, find employees, and increase their business through LinkedIn. He also owns OTB Video Marketing, a video production company helping clients increase exposure through video marketing.

Rod has developed a comprehensive online class about using LinkedIn called "World Class LinkedIn."

More information about this training can be found at www.WorldClassLinkedIn.com.

For more information about Rod Potter, visit https://www.LinkedIn.com/in/RodPotter and connect with him using the email address RodPotter16@Gmail.com

Helping Our Military Veterans and Veteran Families on the Path to Affordable, Stable Housing
By Ken Lacy

Introduction

After a distinguished military career encompassing both active and reserve duty, and meeting with local organizations that provide assistance to veterans, Ken Lacy came to recognize some common challenges veterans and their families have with achieving a stable housing situation. For a number of years he had been involved in the process of rehabilitating properties for investment. Recognizing these types of rehabilitations can be a significant attribute to the solution of veterans' homelessness, Ken founded the non-profit organization, Veterans Path Up, in 2015. Since it's founding Veterans Path Up has helped over 100 veterans and their families on their path to affordable and stable housing in Charlotte and more recently in other areas around the country.

In this chapter Ken describes common challenges veterans and their families are facing in our communities and how Veterans Path Up is providing a helping hand-up.

From Military Service to Helping Veterans Achieve Stable Housing

I spent a total of 26 years serving in the Navy with 9 years of active duty and 17 years of reserve duty. I have been deployed multiple times overseas and the majority of my time in the Navy was spent as a Navy diver and an explosive ordinance disposal diver. My last deployment to the Middle East was with a five-man Explosive Ordinance Disposal (EOD) team performing anti-terrorism force protection diving. I retired from the Navy reserves in 2013.

Upon becoming honorably discharged, I continued my career in the real estate investment industry. After retiring from the reserves I was invited to a veteran's luncheon here in Charlotte sponsored by Charlotte Bridge Home. During that luncheon all of the veterans are requested to stand up, give their 20-second elevator speech on what they're doing now, their branch of service, and if they are in need of any assistance. After the luncheon, one of the executives at Charlotte Bridge Home approached me and said, "We need to put veterans in your homes," and that began the journey of Veterans Path Up.

The Charlotte area has a number of non-profit agencies that are helping veterans get into rentals; however, the housing assistance is for a finite period of time. I began working with service agencies, primarily including Community Link, Charlotte Bridge Home, The Alston Wilkes Society, Crisis Assistance Ministry, Salvation Army, and Family Endeavors. In early 2014 I was approached by The Alston Wilkes Society regarding assistance in placing a mother of two who served a tour in Afghanistan. She was honorably discharged from the Army, had two jobs, and yet she was living in a women's shelter. She had been a battered spouse, and was about to be evicted from the women's shelter because she had been there with her two daughters too long. She was the first veteran who I successfully placed into a home. What resonated with me was how an honorably discharged military veteran with two jobs could be living in a women's shelter along with her two children. I decided that I needed to be part of something that could help more veterans achieve long-term stable housing.

I began to approach several banks and other lending institutions in the area asking them to donate their foreclosed properties, knowing that I was going to rehab them and put a veteran into them. The answer kept coming back, "We like what you're doing, but you need to be an official non-profit for us to be able to work with you." I really didn't want to go through the process of establishing a non-profit because I expected it would take at least nine months and would require money that I did not have. Through commitment and perseverance I assembled a five-member Board of Directors and together we incorporated Veterans Path Up in July of 2015. One of our key board members, who's a Vietnam veteran himself, and has extensive familiarity of non-profits, completed all the paper work associated with obtaining a 501(c)(3) status. Just six weeks after submitting the original paperwork, approval was granted.

Common Challenges for Veterans

There has been a trend of private sector businesses increasingly showing an interest in hiring veterans after they leave the military service. Many want to reach out since they have a philanthropic goal to hire more veterans. Still, a great deal of the hiring process comes down to the veteran's capabilities and what's in their tool bag at the time they apply for the job. Veterans are typically disciplined, and have a lot of structure; however, much of the time their background doesn't match up well with private sector job openings. For the most part enlisted people have the immediate task of reinventing themselves when they're discharged. This transition is a huge hurdle and many have a difficult time finding a job after leaving service.

Officers have at the very minimum a bachelor's degree, which can typically correlate into a civilian career regardless of what their job was in the military. The challenge is for the enlisted people, and it generally doesn't matter if they were in the Navy, Army, Air Force, Marines, National Guard, or Coast Guard because so many of the military jobs have a specific mission that is unrelated to the civilian world. Some examples include infantrymen, gunners, torpedomen, or a whole host of other ratings and enlisted military designations. Veterans that were in technical positions, maintaining sophisticated equipment and electronics, have a background that resonates better on a resume and employers are more likely to hire that person rather than if you just say, "Well I was in the infantry, jumped out of airplanes, and I worked on Jeeps part-time."

Another challenge that I recognized is that even years after people leave the service, bad choices or unfortunate circumstances can occur that puts the vet and family into a temporary or even a long-term financial bind. This is commonly the case when a veteran is injured and they don't have insurance and can't work for some time, so money isn't coming in to pay for housing or other regular expenses.

In the City of Charlotte there are more than 56,000 veterans that have been identified, and that does not include other adjacent counties, where there are over 135,000 veterans. The sad statistic is that over 70% of veterans are in some sort of financial distress. The need for assistance is great but the resources are minimal.

Giving a Helping Hand to Veterans in Need

Veterans Path Up has a mission to provide affordable stable housing to veterans and their families through the use of shared living, single-family residences, and ultimately a path to home ownership. Our emphasis is to provide housing for homeless, working, and disabled veterans, many of whom do not qualify for long-term support from any government agency. We ascribe to a philosophy of helping those with a hand-up, as opposed to a handout. The core of this philosophy starts with stable housing as the cornerstone to a good foundation. Veterans Path Up also provides a critical link to the veteran by bridging the gap to other supportive veteran's services.

The ultimate goal is getting the veteran and family on the path to self-sufficiency. Veterans Path Up also understands that no one organization can satisfy all needs; it is through the collaborative efforts of like-minded giving organizations and individuals, focused teamwork, and the use of all available resources to accomplish the most positive impact for those in need. Education of available support is important to accomplishing our goals. We are not a charity from an entitlement program standpoint; we want to help Veterans become 100% self-sufficient. We're all about teaching a person to fish as opposed to giving a person a fish to eat.

On the day that we received our 501(c)(3) status, I met with the Charlotte/Mecklenburg Housing Partnership. Realizing what we were attempting to achieve, they donated our first property for us to rehab. We completely rehabilitated the house and a veteran family was able to move into the home in February of 2016.

This particular honorably discharged veteran had a stable job and was working at the same place for over 13 years. He was exercising at the gym and threw his back out which caused one of his legs to become permanently disabled.

Between doctors' bills and temporarily not being able to work, the family was in a financially challenging situation. The family initially approached me well in advance before we founded Veterans Path Up but at that time they had a very low credit score due to their situation. They had a variety of living arrangements: bouncing around staying with friends, with relatives, and hotel rooms for quite some time. Initially I provided some tips on cleaning up their credit score because that is an obstacle to achieving stable housing.

After several months the family contacted me again. They had implemented some of the suggestions that I gave them, and their credit score was now rising. They continued to express their desire in finding a place to live and I continued to work with them as we were building the non-profit entity. As we had started working on the first property I kept thinking that I really wanted them to be the ones to end up with this house. They felt like the goal for them was to have home ownership as opposed to renting for the rest of their lives. They were due to be evicted in January but were able to get extended to February. The home was finished on February 1st of 2016 and they moved in initially as renters as their credit score was not quite high enough yet to qualify for financing.

Over time their credit score continued to rise to the point where they were able to qualify for a VA loan. They closed on their loan in November of 2016 and now they are proud homeowners. They went from being homeless to homeowners in under a year. In addition, the veteran is fully employed, and his wife has been fully employed in an assisted living facility for several months. She also has become an ordained minister and has been acting as the chaplain at the assisted living facility. They've been involved in the community and for the second year in a row they are creating a neighborhood garden in their backyard and other neighbors, including children, are welcomed to come help plant the garden.

According to the police, the crime status in that neighborhood has plummeted since the veteran family moved into the house. There had been a lot of drug activity and that now appears to be gone. It's been a wonderful outcome for a house that for the past four years was boarded up. One home can make a difference!

Much of our assistance comes in the form of education and our connections. One veteran we helped had three part-time jobs, just making ends meet for his family. One of his jobs was as a guard for a private security company. While on duty he was severely injured while trying to detain an unruly visitor with a weapon in the store where he was working. The veteran was knocked out, fell to the ground, cracked his head, and was in a coma for three months. While in a comatose state, the family lost all their means of income, his wife and three children were evicted from their home, and were placed in a women's shelter. When the veteran finally woke up, he was released from the hospital and placed into a men's shelter.

The family was able to qualify for a voucher that provides some housing assistance. These vouchers are reserved for honorably discharged veterans, under the HUD-VASH program that is administered by the Charlotte Housing Authority. HUD-VASH stands for Housing and Urban Development Veterans Administration for Supportive Housing. These vouchers are for low-income veterans that qualify based on specific financial needs and are similar to

Section 8 housing vouchers that provide for rent assistance. There's a long waiting list of veterans that have applied for HUD-VASH vouchers and once issued the recipient must use it within six months or it will become void. The vouchers essentially provide for 100% of the rent, and property owners typically will consider the amount of the voucher as part of the income to satisfy a 3-to-1 income to rent ratio. VASH vouchers are available in many cities across the Untied States.

Due to their financial situation this family had difficulties finding a residence that property owners would let them move into. They were approaching the six-month time limit to use the voucher and if they were unable to use it they would be put back on a waiting list that may have hundreds, or thousands of people. At the five-month and two-week mark they were referred to me, which gave them only two weeks left or they were going to lose their voucher. We were able to locate a place for them to move into with a property management company owned by a member of our Board of Directors. They were placed into a house in less than two weeks when the organization that they received the voucher from could not place them in one. As this is being written the family has been in stable housing for two years now.

Sometimes we help with practical financial education. One veteran seeking our assistance was working at a relatively low paying job in a restaurant and was living in a men's shelter. It cost him about $200 per month to stay in the shelter and he was interested in finding more conventional housing. He had an idea of the type of place he would like to move to, but since it would cost about $550 per month for rent, he was having difficulty figuring out how he would be able to afford the rent. I asked how much he was able to save in order to afford the rent. He indicated that he was able to save only about $50 or $100 per month, spending the balance of his income. He actually had a gap of at least $250 per month that he had to reduce in his spending just to be able to afford the rent. I pointed out that he needed to find the difference someway, either by increasing his income or spending less each month to afford the rent. A light bulb seemed to go on in his head as he began to realize what he needed to do.

This particular veteran was provided some assistance through SSVF, Supportive Services for Veteran Families, which would pay a security deposit and three to five months rent, but I suggested he get his financial situation in order so he wasn't just set up for failure a few months down the road when the subsistence support was no longer being offered. As I worked with him over a six-month period he did well in his job and received promotions and small raises. He also stayed on the plan and got control of spending to a point where he could move into a new place.

Veterans Path Up's model is centered around offering a helping hand to our veterans. Because of the fact that we are turning unused properties into income producing properties, or selling them to veterans, we are a unique form of non-profit organization. The Veterans Path Up model moves towards a self-funded organization once enough Veterans are becoming homeowners, and closing on their loans. We've been vetted by the City of Charlotte and other organizations to acquire surplus properties at a low cost. It typically takes less than $50,000 to rehab a property in order to place a veteran in it. The objective is to sell the property to the veteran, which allows us to liquidate the short-term debt that Veterans Path Up has incurred rehabbing the home.

We were able to acquire our second house for a very reduced amount and we completed the rehab not long after the first one. A Vietnam veteran moved into that house, initially as a renter. He had never previously used a VA loan, or any type of home loan for that matter, and in November 2016 he closed on his VA loan and became a homeowner for the first time. Once again Veterans Path Up had a loan against the property that had to be paid off.

Our third house was donated by the City of Charlotte. We partnered with Home Depot on the rehab. Home Depot gave us a $22,000 gift card that paid for about 95 percent of all the materials to rehab the house. The veteran that moved into this house had been working full time at an HVAC company, but was living in his truck right up until the time he moved into the house. He's working on becoming an owner and in the first five months right after moving into the house as a renter he saved significant funds towards his down payment. In the entire neighborhood there's only one other owner-occupant so he will become the second current homeowner in the neighborhood. This was another case of a boarded-up house that is now an asset to the neighborhood. At the same time we were able to help a hard-working veteran, who was homeless, achieve stable housing. The veteran in this property will not be qualified for his loan until 2018 as we continue to work on his credit. Veterans Path up has a $43,000 loan against this property that we must pay off in November 2017.

Home Depot has committed to provide up to $25,000 in funding to Veterans Path Up in Charlotte every quarter in the form of a material gift card. This will allow us to scale up to one house per quarter in partnership with Home Depot.

Veterans Path Up is a solution-centered organization. There are a lot of moving parts and many times there are a lot more things going on in a veteran's life that impacts their ability to have stable housing. The average person that has a job and good credit doesn't even think about this. With poor credit you're not going to get a loan for a house, you're going to pay more for rent, and you're going to pay more for the money that you borrow. This creates a domino effect making it difficult for veterans, or anyone else, to get back on their feet. The veterans we help are interested in being productive members of society, pay their bills, and simply need a hand-up as opposed to a handout.

Since our official founding we have helped over 100 veterans and their families in some way through counseling; and through our various efforts we have helped over 40 veterans in the greater Charlotte area achieve stable housing from a renter's perspective. Our rehab projects are limited by funding and thus far we have completed or have underway 5 rehab projects in Charlotte, resulting in veterans renting or owning the properties. The veteran and family stories listed above are just to provide some examples of our early efforts here in Charlotte.

As we spread the word about what we are doing in Charlotte, there's been an increasing interest around the country about our work. I've been able to make a lot of connections among real estate investors, who many times are already focused on housing rehab projects, so they have the skills and the contractor networks necessary to manage the projects. As a result, we have recently formalized a national Veterans Path Up organization, a framework for chapters to organize in other areas, aligning with our national organization.

A Marine veteran who happens to be a successful real estate investor in Richmond, Virginia has organized the first chapter outside of Charlotte. He has a commitment from the City of Richmond to initially donate 12 houses for rehab. Additionally, he has commitments from two adjoining counties for 17 more properties. He's also put a process in place where a number of local contractors are donating their services and materials for rehabbing the properties.

As this is being written we have also recently added new chapter in Jackson, Mississippi. On the horizon we will have chapters in Dallas-Fort Worth and Houston, Texas; Gary, Indiana; Atlanta, Georgia; and Detroit, Michigan.

As we were starting one of our latest rehab projects in Charlotte we posted information on Facebook, showing the over 50 volunteers that came out to help gut the house and remove brush in the backyard. The post received a lot of attention and was noticed by the Chief of Staff of the Department of Housing and Urban Development (HUD) in Washington, DC. The senior staff member called me to learn more about our organization and at the end of the call asked what HUD can do to help. I'm not sure at this point what the outcome will be with respect to any assistance from HUD, but it's heartening to understand that they seem to appreciate what we are doing to help veterans achieve stable housing with a cost effective model.

In summary, we believe that achieving stable housing is a key ingredient that sets the foundation for a veteran's future success. Our unique model is cost effective and provides a helping hand-up as opposed to a handout. Veterans Path Up rehabs are purposely designed and constructed at a high quality level so that the veteran occupant/owner will not have to worry about maintenance for at least 5 years. This foundation not only sets up the veteran for success, but at the same time increases the pride of ownership in the community, decreases crime, and transforms vacant housing into assets in their neighborhood.

We do have a number of people that donate their time and effort to the organization including doing part of the rehabs; however, our most pressing need is more funds to allow us to scale up to multiple concurrent rehab projects for veteran housing. We encourage people that are interested in helping us in our quest to assist more veterans achieve stable long-term housing to visit our website and make a donation of any amount. Veterans Path Up is online at http://www.VeteransPathUp.org.

About Ken Lacy

Ken Lacy had a distinguished career in the United States Navy and then in the Navy Reserves. His specialty was as a Navy Diver and an Explosive Ordnance Disposal (EOD) diver. He served in multiple deployments to the Middle East in support of underwater anti-terrorism force protection.

After 26 years of active and reserve service, Ken retired from the Navy reserves in 2013 and he decided to devote considerable time and effort in helping his fellow veterans establish stable housing, a considerable need in the greater Charlotte area.

Ken founded Veterans Path Up, a 501(c)(3) non-profit organization in 2015 and he is the Executive Director of the organization.

The mission of Veterans Path Up is to provide affordable stable housing to veterans and veteran families through the use of shared living, single-family residences, and ultimately a path to home ownership. The emphasis is to provide housing for homeless, working, and disabled Veterans many of whom do not qualify for long-term support from any government agency.

For more information about Ken Lacy and Veterans Path Up visit,
http://www.VeteransPathUp.org
https://www.LinkedIn.com/in/KennethLacy

Digital Transformation for Established Companies
By Curtis Hughes

Introduction

Curtis Hughes has a computer science background and after college he was focused on building a variety of software solutions. In 2002 he co-founded C5 Insight, a Charlotte-based IT consulting firm that helps a variety of organizations primarily in financial services, manufacturing, and the energy sector improve employee collaboration, engagement, and customer relationship management. During his fifteen years with C5 Insight, Curtis had the opportunity to help hundreds of midsize and large companies transform their information management and collaboration processes. In early 2017 he joined Midrex Technologies, Inc., as Chief Information Officer (CIO). Midrex is based in Charlotte, North Carolina and is the world leader in designing and building direct-reduced iron (DRI) plants. In his new role, Curtis is using the experience gained over the past twenty years in consulting to develop and implement new technology strategies for Midrex. In this chapter Curtis describes information management challenges often facing well-established companies and the necessary elements for a digital transformation.

From Consulting with a Variety of Organizations to Digital Transformation for One Company

With my background in technology, I've always tried to find more efficiency in everything I do, and if I had to do something twice manually, I tried to figure out a way to automate it. I'm wired to not do tedious things over and over and over. It was a marriage between knowing how software can and should work from a very technical standpoint, and knowing that it should make people more efficient and effective. My philosophy is that we should be able to get more out of technology: leverage it to do the things we want, without constantly being interrupted by it getting in our way. The best technology is invisible technology.

In recent years, I also noticed the existence of a significant link between the software tools being used and employee engagement. In many organizations, employees are disengaged, which ultimately affects customer satisfaction, customer engagement, and the organization's bottom line. In 2002, Geoff Ables and I co-founded C5 Insight, a consulting firm that helps companies improve employee engagement and customer relationships. We utilized technologies such as SharePoint, Microsoft Dynamics CRM, and Salesforce in these initiatives, but we found that it's not all about the technology. Instead, it's also the interaction and engagement of the people in the organizations that make everything work. In fact, most technology projects fail because technology is overemphasized. Over the years, we developed a philosophy called the 40/20/40 Principle, which has helped hundreds of organizations become more successful in their implementation of technology by changing the focus to people and process instead of technology.

After working with hundreds of companies and seeing firsthand what worked and what didn't work, I recently joined Midrex Technologies, Inc. Midrex is interested in developing and implementing new strategies for information management, and I am responsible for leading that initiative in my new role as Chief Information Officer. Like many companies, the CIO role has transitioned from primarily a position that oversees information management infrastructure to forming a partnership with the business and overseeing the IT strategy for the organization.

Information Management Challenges for Established Companies

The amount of data in today's digital world is exploding, and it's a challenge for most businesses to find, interpret, and obtain any useful insight from their data. According to a study by IBM, (Ref: https://www-01.ibm.com/common/ssi/cgi-bin/ssialias?htmlfid=WRL12345USEN) 90 percent of the world's data was created in just the last two years. We're creating so much data at such a rapid pace, yet only 3 percent is actually tagged and easily accessible. In addition, a Gartner study back in 2014 (Ref: http://www.gartner.com/newsroom/id/2672515) predicted that by 2017 — this year — a third of the Fortune 100 companies would experience an information crisis because they couldn't effectively value, govern, and trust their enterprise's information. As a result, such an abundance of data exists that it's all become digital noise. In other words, if *everything* is important, then *nothing* is. The truth is that a lot of organizations continue to accumulate data, without pausing to put together a strategy that will convert that data into actionable information and real knowledge to make better and faster decisions, to help them gain a strategic advantage.

Peter Drucker said, "We spent the last 30 years focusing on the T in IT, and we'll spend the next 30 years focusing on the I." The interesting thing is that he said this back in the '90s, and it's still applicable today, because so many companies are still focusing on the technology, not the information.

Over time, as companies saw a need, they invested in multiple technology solutions without thinking much about the long-term implications, integrations, or investments of that technology. With an accumulation of many systems that perform specific functions but that are not integrated into a whole, an organization simply has bits and pieces of the puzzle that don't work well with each other and are typically very inefficient. There may be hundreds of such systems across a large enterprise, and with the focus on technology, valuable data is being generated at a rapid rate. However, most often, it's simply a vast digital landfill, in which it's nearly impossible to find anything of value. Most companies don't even actually know what they have. When data is stored in a variety of different places and is not classified in a logical manner, it's a lot more difficult to find. When organizations can consolidate information in a common location where it is combined, classified, and organized in a way that is both meaningful and makes sense, the business can then find patterns in the data. The missing component is usually an overall strategic vision for the way in which all the tools and technology *work together* to unlock information.

When an organization operates in the same manner over years or even decades, the employees typically tend to resist change. Of course, this depends on who's leading the organization, but I often hear something like, "We've always done it this way." The reality is that just because the way you've worked for the last 20 years has been successful, it doesn't mean it will work for the next 20 years. Sometimes, the easiest path is to do nothing all because everyone seems to be happy; after all, it's a large business, and to change would be a massive undertaking. The problem is that every industry has companies looking to gain market share by being more efficient, providing a better customer experience, or completely disrupting the industry with completely new ways of doing business. Standing put and resting on a legacy are pretty big risks to take in today's business landscape.

On the other hand, leadership at some companies realize they need to change and embrace new technologies. They have heard about "digital transformation," and that becomes their goal. Or at least they have some recognition that they need to change; however, they need to think of digital transformation as a tool, not a target, because it's just a buzzword. Without even being able to define what a "digital transformation" means, a lot of companies experience paralysis by analysis, or worse, even start moving in the wrong direction.

Company culture plays a big role in how an organization changes and transforms. Millennials and the younger generation in more of a startup mindset comprise the smaller companies I've worked with. They were generally quick to adapt and didn't fear change; in fact, they likely embraced change and didn't fear failure. Established companies that have been around for decades, on the other hand, typically have a wide range of generations represented, from people nearing retirement to millennials and others just graduating from college. Transformation at one of these types of organizations involves a lot of work, and most importantly, it impacts *the way* people work. As a result, for the most part, people in more established companies tend to be more resistant to change.

Keys to Successful Digital Transformation

Transformation requires change, and a company should have some specific reasons for change and a vision of what change means. At this point, many established companies realize that, over the years, they have generated a large accumulation of data. But data without context is not valuable. Data must be transformed into relevant information, which leads to knowledge and ultimately provides actionable insight. So, the reason for change may be to unlock all the accumulated information and use it to provide insight as to how to provide a better customer experience, become more efficient, or increase revenue. Of course, it's important to start with specific issues, not a general question like, "How can we do things differently?" Start with the pain points that are holding back the enterprise. In short, data, information, or knowledge, is not enough; indeed, you must be able to take clear action from the information, a vital point that most organizations miss.

It's a simple but powerful concept to get back to the basics and discover the "Why" when contemplating change. People tend to get caught up in in all the terminology related to digital transformation or information technology and wonder where to start. Start by exploring *why* you are doing what you are doing. How do you discover all your data and uncover the information you currently possess? Why do you want to change in the first place? What, specifically, are you trying to improve or overcome? What do you want the results to look like? What's the business case for making a change? What's the upside potential if you make a change? Or, one of my favorite questions: What happens if you do nothing at all?

This is an ideal time to consider opportunities to organize data to find underlying patterns that can improve the business. Can you easily understand who is buying your product or service? In some cases, the business may have difficulty in seeing the relationships among products that their individual customers are purchasing. For example, they know the total sales of Product A and Product B, but they can't clearly see that almost all customers of Product A are also buying Product B, and few others are buying Product B. By acquiring an ability to recognize the patterns in the customer-buying process, they decided to package the two products together and eliminate the individual products, simplifying the product mix. While studying ways to improve through change, consider the ways that better organization of the data can provide actionable information to fundamentally change what the business is doing. Sometimes, it's the foundations that need to change first. A house built on a foundation that cannot support it will not last.

By peeling back all the layers and discovering *why* you want to change, what you are trying to achieve, and what the final destination looks like, you can develop a vision for what digital transformation means to your organization. Define measurable goals and put together a road map of the process. Just like a road trip from New York to Los Angeles, you can take many possible routes, but if you don't choose a definite course of action and make sure you're staying on it, it's hard, if not impossible, to reach your destination. If the business has 50 or 100 different systems, a clear strategy and road map in place will help figure out how to get everything working consistently in progressing toward that destination.

It's also critical to focus on the people, workflow, and processes, not necessarily the technology products. In other words, the most successful digital transformations always take into account the "non-digital" aspects of the business. Consider what you're trying to do and how it's going to impact people and actually make their jobs easier and allow them to be more productive. My philosophy is to spend about 80 percent on people and process and about 20 percent on technology. By contract, the typical organization spends at least 50% of their time on technology, 25 percent on people, and 25 percent on process. If you can get the people and processes right, the technology's the easy part. Once you understand the requirements, then you can figure out what types of technology will provide the solutions. If you don't focus on the people, processes, and change management, you may just be taking a bad process or a group of people who don't want to change and putting them into a nice, new, shiny system. Then all you have is a bad process that, although it looks good, lacks substance.

Take into consideration how different people work and make sure your system accommodates their differences. Today, everyone's busy and constantly being bombarded by digital noise on phones and tablets. I recall seeing a statistic that while in the office, most employees are only at their desk about 50 percent of the time. How is your system going to accommodate mobile access to important information? Most organizations allow telecommuting, work from home, and work from anywhere, so, how are you adapting to these new ways of working? Another point is that we have a big generational shift in the workforce. The millennials and other younger generations grew up with the internet and digital technology at their fingertips. How is the system going to accommodate how they work? Will you even be able to attract younger people to work at your organization if you don't adapt?

Buy-in from top-to-bottom is also crucial. Engagement needs to start at the top of the organization, so everyone below can see leadership and department heads leading by example. Communication is important to make sure everyone understands they all are on the same bus and moving in the same direction. There needs to be 100 percent clarity of the vision, the road map, how the changes will affect individuals, and the business case for the change. It takes time to get everyone working together toward the same purpose, and it may slow down the initial steps. However, it's better to understand and work on the people side first, before the technology.

In my experience as a consultant or in my role of CIO, when transformation is proposed, I've observed three general types of people. It's important to identify these people and their respective roles, all the way from the top to the user level. First are the "champions," those people who embrace the change or project and who will play key roles while rolling out the project delivery.

I call another group the "lurkers," those who are not against the change, but they are unsure about supporting it and who intend to stand back and see how it goes before embracing the change or getting involved. You've got to focus on this group as well to understand their uncertainties or challenges and what is causing them to not fully get on-board. Maybe they have ideas that haven't been considered, and those ideas may be part of the problem. You've got a better chance of success if you can address their issues and turn them into supporters from the outset.

Finally, there's always another group, the resistors, those people who — no matter what you say — will be against the change. It's important to identify these resistors, so you can make sure they're not preventing forward momentum, or worse, infecting other parts of the organization by spreading negativity.

One of the more important elements for project success is often forgotten — a process for ongoing project review and feedback among both users and stakeholders. Usually, the project is considered "complete," and now it's on to the next project. But is the project still providing the value that was anticipated when it was originally envisioned and implemented? Forget about considering a project "done." Set up a steering committee for all IT projects and meet every quarter for an hour to determine if the system is still working and being utilized to its fullest capacity. Business models and needs change, but has the system changed to accommodate those changes? It's a small amount of time — four hours per year — compared to the investment made in the system. These reviews are also a time to discover if users have any new ideas that will improve adoption and usage, and deliver value. It's like keeping your hands on the wheel while you drive. If you don't check in on it, the system is more likely to begin to die — and people will stop using it.

In summary, there's an abundance of data available within all businesses, but it is rarely organized into easily retrievable and actionable information. Too often companies want to digitally transform their organizations into the modern era of information management and they view technology as a "magic bullet" that will fulfill this vision. With a focus on technology, rather than the people and the processes, most digital transformation projects fail to meet even modest expectations. In working with hundreds of organizations, I've found that the most successful technology projects always consider the non-digital aspects and my philosophy is to spend 80% of the effort on the people and processes. Once these aspects are right, selecting and implementing the technology is the easy part.

About Curtis Hughes

Curtis Hughes is the Chief Information Officer for Midrex Technologies, where he is responsible for defining and executing the company's global technology strategy across more than 20 countries worldwide.

Prior to joining Midrex, Curtis spent nearly two decades as a trusted business leader and technology strategist for corporations and government agencies across North and South America, Europe, Asia, and the Middle East. During this time, he founded or co-founded three companies, the most recent being C5 Insight, a management consulting firm named twice to the INC 5000 list of fastest growing privately held companies, where he served as Managing Partner.

He spends most of his days at the intersection of people and technology, and frequently shares his experience by writing on leadership and technology trends, and speaking at business and technology conferences around the world. He previously served in a leadership role for the Information Technology Advisory Council (ITAC) for the American Red Cross, and currently sits on the Board of Advisors for the UNC Charlotte College of Computing and Informatics (CCI), and in 2012, was named as one of Charlotte's "40 Under 40" in recognition of his business accomplishments and commitment to the community.

Helping Entrepreneurs Develop Successful Businesses
By Torie Mathis

Introduction

Torie Mathis has an interesting story about how she became a successful entrepreneur and in turn is using what she has learned to help other business owners and entrepreneurs achieve their own success. Torie began her career in the U.S. Army and as a result of an accident while serving overseas she had the opportunity to explore different avenues for her work life. Although it was not obvious to her at the time, she discovered that she had a lot of aptitude for commercial design and marketing. Although she had considered teaching as a profession, Torie soon embraced her strengths and earned a degree in advertising.

After working for a publisher of real estate magazines until the big real estate crash several years ago, Torie started her own commercial design and strategic marketing agency. Her desire to help her clients grow their own businesses, led to an expansion of her role into business coaching, helping entrepreneurs and business owners develop their own successful businesses.

In this chapter Torie tells her story of her progression from military service to becoming an entrepreneur helping business with design and strategic marketing and then into business coaching. She offers lessons she learned along the way and offers insights on overcoming common obstacles that frequently get in the way of progress.

From the U.S. Military to Commercial Design and Strategic Marketing

I joined the U.S. Army when I was 21 years old as I was having difficulty self-financing my college education and I really wanted to travel and do something different than stay in the town where I was living. The military seemed to be a good choice for me, as I would get an opportunity to see and live somewhere else. Also, since I eventually wanted to go back to college, the military helps vets with their education expenses. I was stationed in Germany and served there for three years, which was a fantastic experience. My duty was mostly administration and I started volunteering in the community, teaching family readiness, and also giving instruction on making PowerPoint presentations. I really enjoyed the teaching and volunteering work.

While serving in Germany, I broke my hip and I had to leave the military. I was devastated as I had planned a military career and I wasn't ready to just go back home at that point. I had all these dreams and I really enjoyed living in Europe and being in the military and wasn't ready to stop that part of my life. I was fortunate to be able to find a civilian Army job in Germany and stayed for another two years. During that time, I went through the VA rehabilitation program and also received some testing and counseling about my best fit for further education and career opportunities. Although I believed my interests were in teaching, the testing showed I was a great fit for commercial design.

I came back to the states and attended the Academy of Art University in San Francisco and received a degree in advertising. What started off being just a horrible experience that turned my whole life upside down, ended up probably being one of the greatest experiences and opportunities of my life and I was able to receive a fantastic education.

I got what most would consider a "great" corporate job near the end of college. I was making more money than I ever had, but I wasn't using any of the skills I had learned in college. I didn't want to be one of those people that spent all this time and money on a specific degree to never use it. I had a $100K education in design and marketing strategy and I was mostly doing data entry. I found a part-time job making minimum wage as a production assistant at a real estate magazine across town. It was a dream job and I took it, and the huge pay cut.

The real estate market was booming and I moved up to the assistant publisher's position. It was a very fast-paced business and we were publishing about 45 magazines a month at that time. Then there was the big financial collapse and the real estate industry went from booming to almost non-existent. Our 45 magazines a month went down to only four in about three months because everybody had stopped advertising. I had to layoff my production team and we did everything we could just to save the business. At the end of the day, the entire company went under. They decided to completely close the doors and just give it up, but we still had a few clients. Another company picked up the printing and the four clients and they asked if I wanted to stay on to continue doing the production.

I was already working virtually, so I made the decision to start my own business right then. I started with those four clients and acquired a couple of others. I asked everybody I knew or met if they needed any design work and gradually added new customers to fill my time and grow my business.

Over a number of years we have added some large corporate clients as well as many small business owners as clients. For many of the smaller clients we work as a virtual marketing department. We do everything from logo design and websites to strategic marketing consulting and coaching. We design and deliver printed marketing materials like brochures, catalogs, and flyers. We have trade relationships with some large printers around the U.S. so we can get our clients' printed marketing materials done rapidly with a very high quality and at a reasonable cost. Sometimes we are even called in to rescue websites that the clients have been locked out of because of unprofessional design, a missing freelancer, or being hacked.

Lessons Learned Along The Way

I've learned as an entrepreneur, especially with a small business, it's always important to find a better way of doing things, continuously making your processes more efficient. As the saying goes, "Work smarter, not harder." Sometimes this means simply to try different ways to accomplish what you need to get done. We can get a bit uncomfortable when we try something different, but it's amazing the time and the energy that can be saved trying something different that might be better or quicker. Today, a lot of people call finding better methods "hacks," but it's not cheating the system; it's really about being as efficient and effective as you can be.

When I was in the Army, I found a love for the tradition and camaraderie, but my desire to find better ways to do things didn't fit with the standard military protocol. They didn't really care if we came up with a way to save two hours, or even two days, on a task because they had a manual for everything, and we were expected to follow the manual, not invent better methods. This can also be a challenge in some corporate jobs.

The people that are innovative are the ones that are changing the world and building amazing products. I learned to think out of the box a little bit and not be afraid of what other people think. I also learned to have confidence in my direction and not to be afraid of the person that is telling me that maybe I should do something else. I also found that I could not be afraid that I was going to fail or that something was not going to work. It's okay if something doesn't work, but keep on trying to find the solution or answer that results in a better way.

Even before I was an entrepreneur I worked for a few small businesses including my dad's well drilling business. Small businesses appreciate creativity and finding better ways and little shortcuts that make the customer experience better. I learned that people coming out of the military or corporate America could just break out and be bold. It's okay to try and do different things and not be afraid. If you're afraid, just push through the fear and experiment.

We all have an amazing power and control of our lives. We all have the ability to create the life and the lifestyle that we want, and if we can just honestly ask ourselves what we want from life, we can have it. You have to figure out what it is and map it out. One has to think about what an ideal day looks like and then go about and plan to make it happen.

Not having enough time is a very common excuse that people use when dealing with their challenges moving toward success. I regard the concept of time being the obstacle as sort of a "gateway drug." There's no face to time. It's easy to blame time because it's hard to blame ourselves. People will say that they don't have enough time, but we need to see what is really behind the time problem, the root causes, so we can discover the blocks to growing our business. Every one of us humans on earth has the same 24 hours in a day. Nobody is given extra hours. It's how the same 24 hours are used that makes the difference. It's amazing how some people seem to have it all, a great business life, a great family life, a great social life, and they sleep and eat well, and get so many things done. It's a case of using time to the best advantage.

Coaching Entrepreneurs Toward Success

Although it wasn't intentionally planned, my design and marketing business led me into coaching entrepreneurs, both women and men, who are stuck or having issues that are preventing them from growing their businesses. A lot of people with start-up businesses come to us for marketing help. They generally have a business that hasn't been able to get off the ground and they recognize they need to be a little bit more professional and add some marketing to grow their business. It may initially be something like a logo design, an email campaign, or a new website. As we are completing the marketing projects, I observe some other underlying issues that are preventing them from growing the business other than just the marketing. Many times we can see this because the client is not timely executing the marketing programs we have delivered, so there seems to be something else that is also blocking the path to success. It might be a time issue, which might turn into a family issue, or not getting enough sleep, or not eating well.

What starts as a time issue is usually a deeper issue like their success or money mindset or a fear of success for them, or a family member.

One of the best ways to illustrate the type of patterns I frequently encounter is to describe an actual client situation. One of my clients was very creative and had just started a hand-made jewelry business. She contacted me to design a logo and develop a website with some e-commerce. Our implementation required her to supply certain information and photos over the course of the project. We set up weekly meetings to review progress and the client kept coming back with her part not being completed. She said, "I'm having a really hard time just getting everything done. I don't have enough time."

I suggested that she first get a good handle on where she's spending her time because it's difficult to understand even your own situation without some facts. A really simple tool that I like to use that's quite eye opening is a time audit. It's a real simple form that for each day of the week has space to fill in the activity performed for every hour. I suggested that she use the form for one week and that we look at the data at the next weekly meeting. When she came back the next week she indicated that she really has a lot of time, but a lot of the time just slipped away by doing nothing productive. She found that a lot of time during the week was spent with her family, not quality time, but watching TV. The total amount of time spent was preventing her from doing what was necessary for her business.

There is a sample time audit form available on my website. The link is http://www.TorieMathis.com/time.

What started off as a perceived need, just for marketing, ended up uncovering some relationship issues that created a significant time demand that prevented enough time to focus on her business. She said that her husband said that he really supported her business. He was saying, "Go for it. I want you to do this," but what she realized is that he was making her feel bad because he wanted her to sit on the couch in the evenings and watch TV with him. That's normal for a lot of married couples, but that was many hours in a week that she was spending with her husband watching TV, not getting anything productive accomplished.

It seemed like her husband and also her children had a fear that her business was going to overtake her family. She didn't want to go so far out that she was neglecting her family, but she realized that she had to spend enough time with the business or it would fail. I didn't tell her what to say. We just talked about it and it really gave her a sense of empowerment. She was able to say to her husband, "If you are going to support me, then this is what I need to do with some of my time." She was able to set up a schedule that both she and her husband felt comfortable with.

She set up some boundaries so that she could be successful and so that she could be a great mom and wife as well. By talking her through this and setting some healthy boundaries for herself and her business, she was able to compartmentalize both of them and give them both the space they needed to grow and to thrive. That was the beginning of a coaching engagement with her that helped her enjoy both business and family success. Once we figured out the "time" issue, we could move on to strategic ways to increase profits in her business.

I worked with the jewelry design client for several months coaching her toward success in business as well as personal life. She is also part of a military family, which was close to my heart. On top of everything, her family is moving every couple of years and we set up a program for her to continue the exercises used during the coaching engagement. Although our coaching work is finished, and she has moved out of the area, every once in a while she'll email me and tell me that she still uses the different exercises, balance formula, and time audit to stay focused. She's gone off into the world and has become very successful. Her jewelry is in multiple stores around North Carolina and Texas now.

Fear of Failure, Self-Doubt, and Implications of Success

Fear of failure is an unexpressed block for many people. The reality is that everyone is going to fail to some extent and failure is actually good because you're learning through failures. Try a lot of different things and fail early and often. That's how you learn what is working and not working. Sometimes, particularly with women, there is a feeling of uncertainty and self-doubt that seems to get in the way. This may come from a feeling of "not good enough" or that one doesn't deserve the success.

Although being successful is a usual goal for an entrepreneur, the implications of success can bring out another fear. Some people fear the complexities and responsibilities that arise with a business, especially a successful business. Success may imply the need to get an office, to buy office furnishing, and to hire employees. This may fit what is thought to be the typical mold, and these are all potential complications for the owner's life.

The reality is that you can have whatever kind of business that you want. The point is to develop your business concept with intention, meaning deciding what business model you want to pursue and then planning it out. When I work with clients that are starting out, I always ask them, "What kind of business do you want? Do you want to eventually have a corporation and have many employees? Do you want a virtual business where you can work from anywhere?" If you intentionally lay that plan out, then you can have whatever kind of business you want. You can run a relatively large business from home and have your kids at home with you. With today's technology you can even work while you travel from a laptop, if that's your desire. By determining the kind of business you want and what kind of life you want, you can make some real intentional decisions from the very beginning.

Most people don't realize the power that they have over their business and personal lives. No matter what your field or industry, you can decide how many hours you want to work, how many clients you want, and the location of your clients. Once you have clarity on the business life you desire, you will feel more in control of your life and empowered to go out and succeed in building the business that you want.

How to Know You Need a Coach

It's easy to see what appears to be overnight success stories and feel like, "What am I doing wrong? Why isn't it happening for me?" What you don't see with a lot of these people that you see achieving success are the struggles that they went through on the way to getting there. It takes consistent hard work, intention, and determination to get your business and life where you want it.

Although it's very common for people to understand the benefits of a fitness coach or a sports coach, not as many recognize the potential benefits of working with a business coach. If one is struggling with accomplishing their business dreams, gaining financial freedom, developing a schedule around the business that balances with family and personal life, and getting the business to the next level, it might be time to consider working with a coach.

If you are considering working with a coach, it's advisable to find a coach with a compatible personality. You can see if you are compatible with a coach by utilizing a free introductory consultation or an online introductory coaching program that most coaches offer. Even if your family is telling you, "You can do this," it's beneficial to hear it from someone that's completely removed from your life that can see things objectively and give you actionable steps.

Some people fear the time commitment, especially those that believe they don't have enough time to accomplish what they are already trying to do. However, as discussed earlier, a simple time tracking exercise can uncover many wasted hours every week that may be a key reason the business is not growing.

Time for coaching can vary by individual and coach, but what I find that works really well is an hour every two weeks over a three to six month period. That's not a lot of time, and it spreads it out with enough time between sessions to be able to measure progress and yet keeps the client on track.

Some people may fear the cost of coaching, especially if a business is already not making or is losing money. As a business coach I won't work with a client that I don't think I can make great strides for within 30-60 days. If a client is serious and ready to make real strategic implementations in their business, and get beyond surface excuses like time, then the ROI can be seen in this short time period. Coaching is NEVER an expense. It's one of the smartest investments any small business owner will ever make when it comes to building a successful business.

Probably the largest fear of hiring a coach is thinking, "I should be able to do this myself." Attempting to build a business alone doesn't make you a hero. Successful people surround themselves with a team that makes them more successful. Most people understand the value of a physical fitness coach or sports coach that can provide that extra motivation, but when it comes to a business coach, some people don't understand the value. Wealthy people have coaches, likely multiple coaches. When you're doing something new or something that makes you uncomfortable, and building a business is going to make you uncomfortable, it's nice to have somebody in your corner that's been there. Often a business owner is so overwhelmed with the day to day that they don't notice the obvious strategic mistakes in their marketing or use of time and resources.

It's valuable for entrepreneurs to get another point of view when their business isn't taking off as planned. One of the most common overlooked issues with small businesses are wasting time on non-profit producing tasks (thus having no time) and trying to talk to everyone with a bland message. When a business tries to talk to everyone, they end up speaking to no one. The first thing I generally ask is, "Who is your target market?" A frequent answer may be something like, "Men and women from 25-65." Not wanting to miss out on a potential customer, business owners use this blanket approach, but to the market it just sounds like, "Hey, all of you, buy my stuff."

When you have a clear idea of who you're talking to you can talk to them personally. An example is a Taekwondo school I worked with. When I asked who their target market was, they answered with the typical, "Parents (men and women) 25-65." As we began to dig deeper, we realized it wasn't men and women, it was moms most of the time. And because Taekwondo is a costly activity it wasn't usually younger families, as they didn't have the disposable income or time for classes for their kids. We also found it was usually families that were already active; that had gym memberships, went to Cross Fit or Yoga sessions, or did martial arts themselves. We began to craft a real target market, one that they could talk to specifically rather than wasting time trying to market a bland message to everyone.

Another problem I often see is using generic jargon or features for the sales message. Many of these features make you scratch your head thinking, "Well, I hope so." Using bland sales messages like, "Quality," "Attention to detail," or "Experienced Team," are not going to up your profits. These product or service features will not make people act or buy from you nor will they get attention in our fast-paced, saturated digital markets.

When it comes down to it, people don't really buy products or services; they buy solutions to their problems. Defining how your offering solves your customer's problem is part of your strategic marketing message and where the magic starts to happen. Every business needs to market strategically; otherwise they are wasting money hand over fist on tactical ads that don't connect, don't sell, and don't produce a measurable ROI.

I love empowering entrepreneurs to build a business they love that gives them the financial freedom they desire. Strategic Marketing is a formula; it's a lock you can open once you hold the key. And it is the key to designing the business of your dreams.

If you are finding difficulty achieving the business results you desire or if you are wanting to create a business defined by your lifestyle goals, and not the other way around, coaching or a strategic marketing program may be the key for you. If you are tired of excuses, ready to take action, or want to see what I have to offer, visit www.TorieMathis.com, or if you are interested in applying for one-on-one coaching, visit http://www.TorieMathis.com//work-with-me.

About Torie Mathis

Torie Mathis served in the U.S. Army in Germany and since 2007 has been working with entrepreneurs and business owners, helping them build their brands. She is the founder and creative director of the strategic marketing agency Lake Shark Media (formerly EPIC Creative Studio). Torie has a BFA in Advertising from the Academy of Art University in San Francisco, California.

Torie has leveraged her life and entrepreneurial experience to help business owners and individuals grow their business and lifestyle through coaching. She is the founder of Integrative Success, where she helps clients create a holistic approach to success. She also coaches entrepreneurs and business owners toward success in growing their business. Torie is currently building an online business school for business owners where she teaches business fundamentals, digital marketing, and success mindset.

Torie lives with her family near Lake Norman in the Charlotte, North Carolina area and serves clients around the world.

For more information about Torie Mathis, visit
http://www.TorieMathis.com
http://www.LakeSharkMedia.com

Risk Protection for Your Business and Family
By David Angel

Introduction

David Angel had a successful basketball career at Clemson University and then in professional basketball both in the U.S. and in Europe. After leaving basketball, he returned to the U.S. and entered the business world, initially selling heavy trucks. He went on to managing a TV and radio station in Western North Carolina.

David's father was a longtime Nationwide Insurance agent, so he experienced a lot of discussions about protecting families and businesses from a variety of risks. Observing how much his father enjoyed his business and the relationships he had with his clients, David realized the insurance industry was where he belonged. When the opportunity arose, he started his own agency, which has grown over the years into a multi-office agency focused primarily on serving clients in the Carolinas.

In this chapter, David provides an overview of risk protection for families, individuals, and business owners. He covers risk management considerations, which apply to almost all businesses.

He also shares some common mistakes and misunderstandings that business owners have related to proper protection of their businesses. David also talks about the value he places in actively being a part of improving the communities when he and his staff work and live.

From College and Professional Basketball to an Award Winning Insurance Agency Owner

After graduating from Clemson University, where I played basketball, I had a rewarding career in professional basketball in both the U.S. and Europe for a number of years. Returning home to America I had learned two languages and more importantly, I gained a completely different perspective on life.

I realized the blessings we have living in this country and the freedoms we enjoy. Opportunities abound here that are not available in most of the world, and it is our choice to choose our destiny and our level of success. We are only limited by our attitude, our work ethic, and our determination.

I believed that service to others went hand and hand with sales, and with this philosophy I began a career selling heavy trucks to farmers, businesses, and fleets in the Midwest. Focusing on their transportation needs first, instead of my commission, served me well and allowed me to find great success with the customer's needs as my goal. I agreed to manage a TV and radio station in the foothills of North Carolina with the same agenda. That is where I met my wife of over 30 years who rewarded me with 3 beautiful daughters.

My dad, the owner of a Nationwide Insurance agency, unwittingly inspired my entrepreneurial spirit. I observed each year how he enjoyed his business, developed trusting relationships with his customers, and dedicated himself to giving back to the community. We had long discussions about the importance of protection for individuals and businesses. I became fascinated with the insurance industry and knew this is what I was meant to do.

Since my father had such a great experience with Nationwide, this was the only company I would consider. Unfortunately, they were not hiring, but one day after several years of interviewing, my persistence paid off. Nationwide called and said, "Our hiring freeze is off. You're the man!" In February of 1991, I started my own Nationwide Insurance agency and never looked back.

When my father retired several years later, I acquired his agency and opened more offices to better serve our clients. More acquisitions followed and a large acquisition allowed us to expand into North Carolina. Today, we have offices around the Carolinas and do business throughout the eastern U.S. Not only were we able to expand our customer and service base through acquisitions, but we also added talented, knowledgeable, and experienced people to our staff. We consider the loyalty and longevity of our staff (some who have been with us since the beginning) as one of our greatest assets and achievements.

A primary focus for us is commercial insurance for small and mid-sized businesses in the Carolinas. By focusing on these types of businesses we are able to take a personal and detailed interest in their risk management. We are also very active in agricultural insurance especially with family-owned farms and related businesses in our farming communities. In fact, we have agents on the road traveling and working with farmers and businesses throughout the Carolinas.

Over the years, I have drawn a conclusion that is a mantra to me, "growth does not necessarily mean excellence." I believe this to be true in any business. Rather than focusing on selling a policy to everyone, I found if we seek out good solid community focused businesses and serve both their personal and company needs, we can do a great job. We do not have a desire to call on large, national corporations with offices outside our service area. Conversely, our clients are medical offices, CPA firms, Artisan contractors, local manufacturers, distribution centers, family-owned farms, retail establishments, restaurants, and other professional, small businesses.

Taking a judicious approach toward customer selection creates a portfolio of top quality customers with a like-minded approach toward their businesses, customers, charities, and community involvement. It is easy to be loyal, work hard and go the extra mile for these clients.

At the same time, we are anxious to assist start-up companies and young visionaries who are courageous enough to act on their ideas. These entrepreneurs face many challenges and few are aware of the type or scope of insurance protection needed.

Risk Management Considerations for Business Owners and Professionals

In the insurance business, I noticed that many business owners used a different agent for each type of risk. For instance, one agent may service health insurance, another life, another for business property and liability, and yet another for personal home and auto. This makes it extremely difficult to manage, not to mention the lack of accountability. In our agency, we take a full service approach by reviewing all the risks on a regular basis to ensure full coverage at an affordable price.

The most important risk management considerations for business owners and professionals generally include liability, protection of assets, loss of business income, employee protection, and benefit programs for employees. Personal liability risk protection is also critical. Should a business owner with inadequate personal coverage injure someone, the business can be affected by its exposure to loss.

<u>Liability</u>

Liability is generally the first and most important risk for any individual or business as it can have an unlimited potential for loss. With an auto, building, or other property, the loss is limited only to the value of the asset. With liability, depending on how badly someone is injured, losses could reach $100,000, $1 million, or even $5 million. Business owners can be sued or held liable for a variety of liability types such as premise liability where a person is injured on your property or in your business.

Business owners generally understand the concept of protecting someone injured on their property, but what about other potential risks? If you sell or service a product, protection against a defective product causing bodily harm is necessary. Advertising and personal injury are other risks. Proper coverage protects the business against infringement, failure to perform, libel, and slander.

Employment practices liability is currently a hot button in lawsuits. Business owners are encouraged to consider Employment Practices Liability Insurance (EPLI) to insure against risk associated with treatment of employees, manner of discharge, and work environment. A related risk is Employment Benefits Liability, providing protection should benefits offered not be fulfilled as promised.

Commercial business and commercial auto liability insurance is an important safeguard for your business. Typically, commercial vehicles are identified by signage creating a sense that more money may be available to settle lawsuits. A serious injury may result in a huge exposure.

One must remember that anyone can sue you so it is vitally important that you are properly protected, as your legal defense is one of the highest expenses you will incur.

Protection of Assets

Assets include real property that is owned and all personal and business property in or on the real property including inventory owned by the business. Typically, property is protected from damage or loss due to fire, hail, wind, and vandalism, but is the property protected from all possible exposures?

Generally, buildings are not covered against flood damage unless they are in a designated flood zone, but weather patterns have become more unpredictable and flooding is occurring in areas not in the 100-year flood zone.

Recently, we have seen unexpected flooding in both Carolinas and throughout the country, most of which were outside the 100 year flood zone. Consequently, we encourage our clients to seriously consider adding flood insurance. Adding flood insurance to property not located in a flood zone is very affordable.

In the past few years, we have seen more earthquakes occurring outside of traditionally active areas like California. We recommend our clients at least consider adding earthquake coverage as an option.

Tangible property is typically covered for risks due to fire, theft and vandalism. Again, are you covered for all types of losses and is coverage for property and inventory extended? How are losses covered when they are away from your business or home? Will inventory be covered as cargo on a truck en route to a customer? You may have two suitcases full of samples worth $10,000 being shipped to an exhibit. If the airline loses the suitcases and your samples do not arrive, are you covered? Are you covered for rising water? If your warehouse has a backup in the sewer or septic system resulting in damage to your inventory, is the inventory covered?

Off-premise power failure is a risk we are particularly concerned with in the Southeast due to the number of electrical storms in the area. Even though your business may not experience a direct hit, a transformer strike in the area could result in power failure on your property. Businesses relying on refrigeration are particularly vulnerable and could be out-of-operation for days.

As part of our standard operating procedure, our agents perform an annual review to assess perils covered, exposures and coverage levels, and especially additions of locations, equipment, or vehicles.

Loss of Business Income

Loss of business income coverage can be critical to your company's future after a loss. For instance, should the building you lease or own burn and consequently be uninhabitable, do you have the funds to move to another building and operate until the structure is repaired or restored? Can you cover expenses for moving, additional equipment, cover regular bills, loans, and continue to pay your employees? We highly recommend our clients obtain Loss of Business Income coverage.

Workers' Compensation

Workers' Compensation insurance is a requirement for business owners. Although regulations vary by state, most require coverage for businesses with four or more employees.

Workers' Compensation protects the employee as well as the employer by providing wage replacement in exchange for mandatory relinquishment of the employee's right to sue. Worker's Compensation pays medical and hospital bills and replaces income for the injured worker freeing the employer from this obligation.

It is important for us to review the job descriptions carefully to properly code your workforce as this, plus payroll, is a determining factor for Workers' Compensation premiums.

<u>Employee Benefits</u>

As the economy continues to recover, good employees are more difficult to find. One of the best ways to attract and retain a quality workforce is through a good benefit program. With cost of health insurance rapidly increasing, employees are more likely to choose companies with a good benefit program rather than accept a small wage increase.

Retirement benefits may be even more important to employees than wage increases. There are many different types of simple retirement plans suitable for small, mid-size, and larger companies. Some of the most popular are a 401K, Simple IRA, and SEP.

Additional individual group benefits can be provided to the employees at no cost to the employer. These include short-term disability, accident policies, life insurance, and cancer policies. These policies are relatively inexpensive as they are provided at a group rate. The employer agrees to a payroll deduction plan for payment and can also participate in the cost if desired.

Common Mistakes in Risk Management

<u>Liability Coverage</u>

An area we try to focus on is maintaining a high level of liability coverage. Probably the most prevalent mistake I see is related to not having enough coverage. We like to educate our clients on the benefit of self-insuring small claims that can be paid by the company or individual, and increasing coverage for events that are not affordable. It is common to see small business owners with only $500,000 of liability with a small deductible. However, increasing coverage to $2 million can be very inexpensive if the deductible is increased to $1,000 or $5,000. In some cases, raising the deductible may pay for the increased coverage. The increase in coverage limits provides maximum protection in case of a catastrophic loss.

Often, I observe business owners or other highly compensated professionals with large liability limits for their business, but carrying minimum limits on their home and auto. They are only an accident away from losing their business because they have exposed themselves personally. From our perspective, we want to align those policies so that liabilities are closed with no open gaps in the coverage. This usually warrants a personal umbrella of additional liability coverage, an inexpensive policy that packs a lot of catastrophic protection.

<u>Coverage of Personal Property</u>

Another mistake we see is assuming personal property is covered and not considering the deductibles or limits of coverage. As an example, people will carry large deductibles on homeowners and business casualty insurance in order to realize premium savings, not realizing that the deductible also applies to losses of personal property. Consequently, losses under the deductible amount will not be covered. A more common issue is not understanding the limits of coverage for various types of personal property. For example, homeowners insurance policies generally limit coverage on jewelry, silver, guns, antiques, camera equipment, and other specific types of property unless specifically scheduled. It is very common to have property that has a higher value than the coverage limit.

We encourage clients to place all special personal property in a separate Inland Marine policy, also called a scheduled policy. Now, the property is not exposed to the large deductible but is covered with no deductible. In addition, when there is a claim, it does not affect your homeowner or commercial policy through increased premiums. This type of policy is very affordable, costing about $10 per $1,000 per year depending on property value. The same applies to business equipment, which may be located or transported on your trucks. This equipment can be covered through a Marine policy and receive the benefit of a lower deductible.

<u>Coverage of New Property or Risks</u>

It is critical to inform your insurance agent when conditions change or new property is acquired to ensure the property and new risks are adequately covered. We insure a high volume of agricultural risks and farmers are always seeking opportunities to acquire additional land. The land may be vacant and does not appear to be exposed to risk, so the farmer tends to wait until the next annual review. However, should someone fall on the property and an injury occurs, the owner or lessor may be liable. The same conditions apply to a builder who acquires lots to hold until construction begins. It is very simple and inexpensive to extend the base policy to include newly acquired land.

How to Select an Insurance Agent

First of all, you want to select an agent representing a top A-rated company. There are many companies you will recognize through endless ad campaigns that have a poor claims record and a low rating. It is easy to find these companies on the Internet and TV. These companies are unable to give individualized service. You will seldom speak to the same person in the large call centers and quite likely find yourself in an overseas call center. The premiums may be cheaper initially, but for sure premium increases will come, and they will provide little or no value when reviewing your personal situation.

Look for someone who can handle your insurance, business, and personal needs. Look for a local agent who will visit your office or home to understand your complete risk situation. Select an agent who has a well-staffed office and is accessible when you need them.

Another consideration is who you will call when you have a problem or will come to your aid when there is a major loss. What support will you receive if the claim is not settled properly or you do not receive immediate response? Who is going to work for you and take care of you? Select a local agent who cares about you and your community.

A good agent will be accountable to you for all things. Your agent should be a person or have a member of his staff who will coordinate all of the business and personal protection together to be accountable to you, the policyholder. It is easier to provide the best advice and guidance when we are taking care of all our clients' personal and business coverage, their homes and cars as well as business coverage, employee benefits, life insurance, liability, and business autos. Our clients may not always know the right questions to ask, but by knowing their entire business and personal situation, we can advise them properly.

An agent is essentially a first line underwriter so it is important the client provide all pertinent information relative to their business or personal situation. Agents are not prying when asking so many questions and since the insurance industry is bound by a privacy act, we are restricted from sharing information. In addition to a lengthy interview, an agent will require a tour of your business or home. Be sure to communicate all exposures honestly. If information is withheld, a loss may not be covered.

When requesting a new quote, an agent may ask for your current policy so as to assure the quote is at least an 'apples to apples' comparison. An experienced agent will still want to perform a complete risk analysis to guarantee you have full coverage. If it differs from your current coverage, then it is easy to compare and justify a new policy.

An agent will give the same personal attention to your personal insurance needs – it would be a disservice to ignore any part of your insurance needs. Remember, if you are the owner or partner of a business, personal liability goes hand-in-hand with commercial liability.

An agent should offer to meet with your advisors such as banker, attorney or CPA. Your agent should be one of your regular advisors, and that relationship will evolve as you grow your business and face different exposures.

In the modern business world, it is rare to speak to a real person on the first attempt. Frequently, you will encounter an automated attendant with a multi-level menu just to leave a message. Confirm with your agent how phone calls are answered, the response time and ease of filing a claim.

Finally, ask your agent to explain what you are NOT covered for as part of your review. You do not want the surprise of calling in a claim and being told, "You did not buy that coverage."

In our office, a live person will answer, not a machine, and properly direct your call. When clients enter our offices, they will be greeted by a member of our staff. Just give us a little time and they will be able to address you by name.

Like many small and mid-sized businesses, our company, agents, and staff support our local businesses and charities.

Through civic events, sponsorship of neighborhood festivals, shopping locally, or supporting favorite charities and youth sports, we encourage participation and are proud of our involvement.

I personally have coached youth sports, chaired fraternal organizations, and served on many boards and committees. Volunteering is a personal decision for me, and one I would make if I did not own a business. It is rewarding when people say, "You coached my kid," "Thanks for working with me on the March of Dimes," "You helped us raise money for Camp Ark," or "You spoke with all the kids about drunk driving." Certainly our business has benefitted from our activities but only as a side effect.

I will close with this message:

I have found that what we give back to our community always comes back to us tenfold. I think this is God's way of reaffirming our efforts for our service to our fellowman given truly from our heart.

I have been blessed being raised in a loving family, and now I have a wonderful supportive wife and three terrific daughters. I am living in my favorite place in the world, doing what I love to do; I am living my dream.

So I ask you, what are you doing to find your happiness?

About David Angel

David Angel is Owner and President of Angel Insurance & Financial Services, Inc., a Nationwide Insurance agency with four offices in North and South Carolina. A graduate of Clemson University, he attended on a full basketball scholarship where he led the Tigers in scoring and rebounding for three years.

After college, he played professional basketball in the U.S. and Europe. Upon returning the U.S., he had a successful career selling trucks and trailers to export, retail and national accounts as well as managing radio and TV stations.

Since 1991, David has been an agency owner representing Nationwide Insurance.

David has grown his agency both organically and through acquisitions in the Carolinas. He has won a number of awards of excellence in the insurance industry including:

- Twice "National Service Agency of the Year"
- Member of "Million Dollar Round Table" – the insurance industry's highest honor
- South Carolina's only member of the "Nationwide Hall of Fame"
- Twice named to "All Star Team" – top 12 agents in America
- Voted "Best Insurance Agency" in Rock Hill by readers of *The Herald* 17 consecutive years
- Awarded South Carolina "Agent of the Year" 18 of the last 25 years

David grew up in a family that was involved in volunteering and local community service, and he has followed that tradition throughout his career. He's very involved with his church, has coached and sponsored youth sports teams, and is involved in a wide variety of community organizations including Optimist, Chamber of Commerce, Worthy Boys and Girls Camp, Children's Attention Home, Cheer for Children, and Come See Me Festival.

David and his wife, Jan, reside in Rock Hill, South Carolina. They have three wonderful daughters who have also been very successful in sports in both college and professional Volleyball, with all three graduating with honors.

For more information about David Angel and The Angel Agency, visit www.AngelInsurance.com

He can also be contacted as follows:

DAngel@AngelInsurance.com
803- 327-6112 (Office)

Financial Planning for Business Owners and Professionals
By Jim Zuelsdorf

Introduction

Jim Zuelsdorf was a small business, owner who observed within his own family the importance of being prepared for financial uncertainties. As he was researching a new career, this experience led him to pursue a field where he could help others prepare for retirement, while at the same time minimizing financial risks for the business owners and their families.

In this chapter Jim provides an overview of financial planning for business owners and professionals, who often are so focused on their businesses that they haven't thought about developing a financial plan for retirement. He explains the keys elements of a financial plan as well as common mistakes business owners and professionals are making with respect to short-term as well as long-term risks.

From Retail Business Owner to Helping Other Business Owners and Professionals Develop Financial Plans for Their Future

Earlier in my career, I was a small business owner with two hardware stores and a Ben Franklin Variety Store. Interest rates were climbing in the 80s, and due to the way my loans were structured, I decided to leave the retail business and research another profession. My father had recently passed without having purchased a life insurance policy and I experienced the effect it had on my mother emotionally and financially. I realized then that many people lack sufficient insurance and financial planning, leaving themselves unprepared for future events. Having the desire to help people reach their hopes and dreams, I decided to enter the financial planning industry in 1986.

For the past three decades, I've been helping people acquire, grow, and protect their wealth. I use the latest financial planning techniques in order to make sure that their immediate, mid-term, and even long-range goals, are met in the most tax-favored and cost effective ways. I'm the owner of Integrity Planning Group in Charlotte, North Carolina, and my clients tend to be small business owners and professionals, 45 years of age or older. Much of my work is in the pre-retirement and retirement planning market, oriented more toward the investment side in addition to extended healthcare management, protection and legacy creation. I help my clients make sure that their visions and dreams are realized and that they can have a comfortable retirement. They may even choose to continue working during retirement - because they want to - not because they must. I also help make sure that everything will be okay whether they live a long life, die prematurely, or become disabled along the way.

Challenges for the Baby Boomer Generation

The biggest challenge facing those of the Baby Boomer Generation is that many haven't saved enough money for retirement and are going to end up working much longer than expected. Another concern is that they will have to compromise the lifestyle they envisioned. Even if an investment plan is in place, there are several potential unforeseen events that can happen to get in the way of funding a successful investment plan.

If a disability occurs, is your business still going to be okay?

Is your family going to be able to continue toward goals you planned together if you die prematurely?

Most people don't factor in the chances of having some sort of disability during their working years, whether it is temporary or permanent. We tend to think that we're not vulnerable to anything because we exercise, eat right, and take the advice of our doctors. Yet there are many things that can prevent the ability to put money away as well as the capacity to earn it. As an example, I was on disability at age 49 because of a cancer diagnosis; it was a short-term situation. It only lasted a couple of years, but had I not had a financial plan in place, the disability insurance wouldn't have left me in the encouraging financial situation that I am today. Because of the plan I had in place, my family never had to worry.

Financial Planning Explained

Financial planning is a comprehensive review of an individual's or a family's financial situation with regard to their unique short, medium, and long-term goals, then analyzing income and expenses to develop a roadmap for achieving those goals. It's difficult to know the direction to take unless you know your destination, so the first step is to understand your immediate goals as they may relate to the distant future. This may include funding college educations, the purchase of a larger house, obtaining a second or vacation home, pinpointing your desired retirement age, and intended lifestyle. Goals should be concrete with a definite timeline to track progress toward the goals. In working with clients to develop their financial plans, many times I help to prioritize their objectives. Very few of us have the unlimited financial resources required to do everything we want simultaneously.

After establishing goals, the next step is an analysis of all your monthly income and expenses to understand your cash flow and determine the amount of money needed for monthly debt service, savings, and investment. Surprisingly, many people don't realize where their money is going. I've had clients over the years that don't even realize what they're spending on monthly services like cable bills, utilities, and subscription services. Many times, monthly service charges come directly out of their checking account or are processed on their credit card; out of sight and out of mind.

Retirement strategy is an important component of the financial plan. It's not only to determine when you want to retire but also what kind of retirement you want. Do you want two houses in different climate zones? Do you want to travel? Then we need to establish a strategy that will enable achieving an independent retirement. This includes the approach for accumulating the necessary amount of capital for retirement and the plan for distribution of the capital over a lifetime. Risk management is another key part of a financial plan. This includes assessing risk exposures and a strategy to put coverage in place to protect a family and its assets from financial loss. Typical considerations include life and disability insurance as well as long-term care insurance. Each can prepare you for a lack of income and the addition of medical costs for care.

Finally, an investment plan is developed which includes customized asset allocation based on your specific investment objectives, risk profile, tax reduction strategies, and capital accumulation requirements. The investment plan establishes criteria for selecting, purchasing, and selling investments as well as a plan to change asset allocation over time. Portfolio diversification is a key factor that must be considered. There are many, many types of investment funds, each focused on different segments such as small caps, large caps, market index, value funds, emerging markets, technology, and more. Diversification doesn't mean buying the same type of fund from multiple companies; it requires different types of assets to be true diversification.

At least in the current environment, estate taxes are not a major concern due to the threshold, but it's important to understand that there still may be a huge tax problem with qualified or tax deferred money. I do a lot of work in that area, helping people make sure that their hard-earned money passes to the correct beneficiary in the most tax-favored manner.

A financial plan may also consider tax planning, estate planning to create arrangements for the preservation and distribution of assets, and review of other risk factors such as personal liability and property and casualty coverage. Specialists such as CPAs, attorneys, residential home and auto insurance agents, and commercial insurance agents, are generally consulted on these parts of the plan.

It's important to periodically review the financial plan against the benchmarks set and to make sure it still accurately reflects your goals and current financial situation. Life happens and conditions change so the plan should be reviewed and adjusted over time. For example, you get an unexpected raise so now you're able to put more money away than we had originally planned.

In my work with clients, we can provide a complete and comprehensive financial plan, or a more limited focus, depending upon the priority. For Instance, some clients want to initially focus on savings for college and get the planning and saving or investment for that underway before tackling other goals.

Common Mistakes

The biggest mistake that I see is not creating a financial plan in the first place. It's pretty common with many professionals and business owners. They're so focused on being successful at their business, or their professional craft, that they often don't see the big picture and overlook developing a financial plan. They may be putting money away, but they don't realize that it's not going to be enough for retirement. They may believe that when they get to retirement age they will have a good sum of money. They may not consider inflation and not understand the amount of money that will be needed for a comfortable retirement allowing them to do the things they planned.

Putting a financial plan in place is an important first step, but I observe many people who don't execute it. They may think they will get to it tomorrow and suddenly, it's five years later and they are still procrastinating. A big mistake is not beginning the funding necessary for the plan and not putting the proper documents in place, such as a will, life insurance, contingency process to transfer ownership, or details regarding financials and continuing the business plan.

Many businesses are organized as partnerships, but I see some that do not have a contingency plan should one of the partners become disabled or die prematurely.

Will your business still be viable?

Make sure you determine who will continue both yours and your business partner's role and interests.

Will that be a surviving spouse who may not share your expertise or ideas?

There may be a buy/sell agreement in place, but often it's not funded or not funded properly. In these cases, if something unexpected happens, the outcome isn't exactly what was intended.

Most business owners haven't thought about business overhead expense insurance. In the event that something would happen due to a health issue or injury, and the owner is not able to go to work or open for business, there can be pretty large ongoing expenses. Business overhead expense insurance can cover many ongoing business expenses such as rent, utilities, wages, interest payments on outstanding eligible business debts, and many other expenses related to running a business.

It's a well-known fact that a great majority of Americans are under-insured when it comes to both life and disability insurance. Most admit they don't have enough life insurance or any at all, yet they don't do anything about it. Disability insurance is also important because it's 60% more likely that you're going to become disabled during your working years as opposed to having a premature death. Unfortunately, many people are not covered for a disability.

Why Hiring a Professional Makes Sense

People can certainly create their own financial plan, but will they actually do it? And do they have the know-how and experience to objectively prepare an effective plan? There's a lot of financial and investment resources available on the internet today, which is both a positive and negative factor due to the sheer abundance of information. It takes a financial professional to wade through all the noise and get clarity on what is important; to provide the insight and advice to develop an accurate financial plan. Some people think that financial planning is strictly investing, and that's a big portion of it, but investing and financial planning without risk management can result in the financial plan going out the window.

Some people think they can pick an investment fund simply by looking at information on past performance year-to-year. I've got a collection of financial magazines and every year their top-rated funds don't repeat the following year. It's important to be able to understand the facts and not be derailed by an impenetrable fog of information.

One of the greatest insights I provide for my clients is to get into an investment mindset where they are paying themselves first, just like a monthly bill. Everyone needs to put some money aside, and if you haven't done it yet, there's no better time to start than now. Working with a qualified financial planner is like having an objective set of eyes checking over all the details. Many people have good intentions of starting an investment plan, but fail to do it on their own for some reason.

I run across a lot of people who have a 401K at work and they're not even taking advantage of the company match. There may be a match of 4 or 5% and they're only investing 1 or 2% because they think that's all they can afford. It's my job to point out to them that they're giving free money away by not at least taking advantage of the match that the employer is willing to provide.

How to Select a Financial Planner

For someone interested in working with a financial planner, it's important first to work with someone they know, like, and trust. Work with someone who's been through full market cycles, one that's been working long enough to have experienced both the uptick in the market, as well as the downturn and volatile times. This is important so that appropriate advice and experience can be provided in uncertain times and corrections can be made when it appears that things aren't working as they should. Understand that investing in volatile or down markets can be a good thing when done in an ongoing professional investment program. It allows you to buy in at a lower cost basis and benefit from market fluctuation.

It's also important that your financial planner has access to a variety of investment and risk management solutions. From an investment standpoint, that means access to mutual funds, annuities, and a full range of independent registered investment advisory services. I provide access to a variety of investment solutions as well as life, disability, and long-term care insurances.

Although I don't provide property or casualty insurance, I have relationships with other professionals that do both commercial and individual property and casualty. I have alliances with attorneys for trust work and to get legal documents in place and contacts with CPAs for both business owners and individuals needing tax planning advice. When any other specialized advice is needed, we bring another appropriate professional into the mix.

Like most professions, there have been unfortunate events in the industry. The Bernie Madoff's of the world have cast a shadow on the investment world and created some apprehension or distrust. Some people view working with a financial professional as one of their largest risks, but over the years my retention rate with clients is almost 100%. Once people do start working with me, they understand that their best interests are first and foremost in my practice. I'm going to make sure that the plan we put in place for each client is the right choice for them and we will continue to adjust it as life happens.

About Jim Zuelsdorf

Jim Zuelsdorf is the owner of Integrity Planning in Charlotte, North Carolina. During his 30 plus years in the Financial Services Industry, he has built a successful Financial Planning practice in Milwaukee, WI and helped in building an agency for John Hancock in the Milwaukee area. Jim has also spent 13 years with Prudential as a regional sales manager and regional Vice President in the Individual Long Term Care department and as a Manager of Agency Training for the Prudential Wisconsin Agency.

Jim is active as a member of the Advisory Board to the Academy of Finance at Olympic High School in Charlotte, NC and a member of the Board of Directors of the Arrowood Business Association, also in Charlotte, NC.

His charities include the American Cancer Society and the Mental Health Association of Charlotte. He is a member of Morningstar Presbyterian Church. In his off time, Jim enjoys gourmet cooking, photography, woodworking, and walking his 2 dogs.

For more information about Jim Zuelsdorf, visit www.IntegrityPlanning.com

Finding the Perfect Nanny
By Dominique Rice

Introduction

Dominique Rice enjoyed working as a nanny for different families over several years. Her career as a nanny was her passion and doing something different was far from her mind. While networking in the industry she realized that there were frequent disconnects between employing families and their nannies. Many nannies weren't happy in their jobs, and a lot of people who employed nannies were not happy with their nanny's job performance. She decided to find a way that both the nannies and the families they work for could find the perfect mutual fit so they could all be happy with the family/nanny relationships. So, Dominique decided to provide the best solution for both nannies and families. Alas, Perfect Fit Placement was created in 2012.

In this chapter Dominique tells the story about how her experience has led her to help families find the perfect nanny and how she facilitates other high quality childcare solutions for busy parents and businesses, as well as helping nannies find the perfect fit in an employer.

Challenges for Busy Parents

Working parents can have a number of challenges with childcare, especially if both parents work or if it is a single-parent family. These can range anywhere from care for an infant or pre-school child/children to care for a child/children when they are sick and out of school for a day. Many professionals have schedules that require some late hours and travel, so typical childcare doesn't always work. Some busy parents also need help with other household support to make life easier when they come home.

A typical need is childcare for a young pre-school child/children when there is not a stay-at-home parent. A daycare facility or a pre-school is not always an option. Not everyone has a traditional nine-to-five job anymore and many jobs require travel or work on differing schedules. Business owners; corporate executives and managers; professionals like doctors, surgeons, lawyers and consultants; professional athletes; and others will typically work long or odd hours and travel is frequently required. Having to stay late due to a work emergency is also common. Most daycares operate Monday through Friday from 7:00 a.m. to 6:00 p.m. and don't have a way to accommodate for any needs outside of their regular hours.

Younger school-age children often attend daycare after school, but the same issues arise if care is needed after the daycare's hours. Even if school and/or daycare hours sufficiently cover the regular needs, when a child is sick and can't attend school or daycare, the parent usually needs to stay home to care for the child/children. This can be a significant issue for some parents who are losing all their income when they need to stay at home. For example a surgeon may have a full day of surgery scheduled that may have to be cancelled at the last moment due to having to stay at home with their child/children. Another consideration is taking care of the child/children when school is not in session – school holidays, summer, snow days, teacher workdays, etc.

A full-time nanny or an on-call back-up childcare professional can be a good solution for busy working parents. Some parents prefer a full-time nanny so that their child/children has one-on-one care right in the home. Additionally, a lot of nannies are able to assist with other household support like laundry, light house keeping, running errands and meal prep.

As I mentioned, professionals may lose significant income and their clients may be affected if the professional unexpectedly has to cancel work due to a child's illness. Businesses are recognizing the same impact of work not getting completed when executives or key employees have to be absent due to an emergency childcare requirement. There are many jobs where one can temporarily work at home, but also many jobs, especially involving sales and service that require personal presence. Recognizing both the personal as well as the business impact when a parent needs to stay at home to care for their child/children, some businesses are now offering a benefit of emergency childcare assistance. This can be very cost-effective for the business and they will typically contract with a qualified agency to provide the back-up care needs of their employees.

Parents can be nervous and afraid when deciding on a childcare solution. A lot of parents are uncertain about the decision, especially mothers, because in most instances the mother is the caregiver. He/she wants to be there at home, but he/she also has to go to work. These are common feelings and concerns thinking about any kind of childcare, whether it's a nanny, a daycare, sending children to pre-school, or to school.

Common Mistakes in Hiring a Nanny

We've observed some typical mistakes that a lot of parents make when searching for and hiring a nanny. They meet with a few candidates and one or more seem to be a good fit based on the personality and the resume presented. It's easy to be convinced to hire a person that seems pleasant and displays what appears to be a good work record. So, based on one or more interviews, the candidate that appears to be great is hired.

One of the biggest mistakes is hiring a nanny without a thorough background check. The person you hire is going to be trusted to take care of the children, generally when no one else is home. What you won't know without a proper background check is if the candidate has a criminal record. He/she may have been a nanny for a number of families in the past, but no one checked the nanny's background. Clearly, you don't want to leave a person with a serious criminal background responsible for taking care of your children.

A similar mistake is not thoroughly performing reference checks with past employers. Again, the nanny may appear to be very qualified based on an interview and a resume, but you really won't know much about the actual work record without talking with past employers. You'll want to find out how he/she got along with the family, if there were any trust issues, what his/her duties were, and the reason why he/she left. A real red flag is if the nanny can't or won't provide references.

Every family's needs are different and there is a wide range of potential duties for a nanny, beyond childcare. As an example, some families have a need for someone to help with meal prep, laundry, or other errands. Work schedule and travel may dictate variable hours being required. When hiring the nanny it's important for both the family and the nanny to have an understanding of all of the expectations on both sides; otherwise there's likely to be some frustration in the future. It's easy to have a verbal discussion regarding all of these aspects; however, a common mistake is not documenting everything in a contract. A written nanny agreement between the family and nanny should outline hours, scheduling, pay, vacation, detail job duties, and everything else that is expected. In this way there is not likely to be any misunderstanding on either side about expectations.

Developing Childcare Solutions for Families and Businesses

Our company, Perfect Fit Placement, is based in Charlotte, North Carolina and is organized to solve four common challenges, all related to childcare:

- Helping families find the perfect nanny to care for their children
- Helping families with back-up, temporary, or occasional in-home childcare needs
- Helping companies provide back-up or temporary in-home childcare for employees
- Helping nannies find the perfect match to families for their employment

Most of the families we work with to find a nanny have one or both parents working as professionals or in senior positions. They may be doctors, lawyers, professional athletes, corporate executives, consultants, and in a variety of fields. Quite a few also have one stay-at-home parent, but are busy and want some help with childcare and possibly other household services. They may be looking for a nanny for the first time or they may have had a nanny that did not work out so they are looking for a more professional approach to finding top-notch care for their children. For the most part nannies do not live in the home; however, in some cases families are looking for a live-in nanny.

Generally we meet with our clients interested in hiring a nanny face-to-face in their home. We want to meet with the families, including the children, so we can really learn about them and their needs. That way when we are recommending candidates for the family to interview, it's not just giving them some resumes, it's recommending one or more great candidates that will be a perfect fit for the family because of needs and personality. We also help the family and nanny come up with a mutually agreeable contract covering all aspects of job expectations, salary, duties, schedule, and vacation. The other thing we do is quarterly check-ins with our clients to make sure the nanny is continuing to meet the family's standard.

We also help families needing back up or short-term care providers. Typically this service is for emergencies when the child/children is sick and not attending school, but it can also help with care when a parent is traveling. Sometimes the care provider will stay overnight for a day or two or even up to a week. Parents that register with us have access to our website to request care and quickly are set up with one of our pre-screened caregivers.

Our corporate service provides the opportunity for employees of companies partnering with us to utilize our back-up care program when they need it the most—when their children are sick, school is closed, their nanny called out sick, or their standard form of childcare is not available. Insightful companies want their employees to be able to come to work; so many have been offering employees a benefit that provides back up, in-home childcare. This not only helps the company maintain consistency in their work, but it's also a great tool for employee retention and is another way to stand out from competitors for employees. We have a range of packages available and we can even include elder care. Once a company partners with us; we enroll their eligible employees over a 30-day period and then launch the service. Similar to the service for families, the employee needing service will go to our website to request service, pick a caregiver best matching their need, and book the care for their loved one.

Whether we are selecting a nanny for a family or selecting a caregiver for one of our other services, we perform the same kind of extensive screening so our clients can feel comfortable with their caregiver. In the first step, a candidate fills out a unique application on our website. The application process includes three assessments: personality, cognitive, and attitude. We have found these assessments screen out a number of people that are not likely to succeed as a caregiver or may not be a good fit for certain families. There are some people that are amazing caregivers, but personality-wise, they may not be able to follow the direction as well as our clients are looking for. Personality screening is also important because some parents and caregivers may have different beliefs that are not compatible and it may be difficult for either to adapt. Cognitive screening is important because in many cases the nanny may be monitoring the child's completion of a school lesson plan and helping with homework. Attitude testing is something we've recently adopted and helps to screen out applicants that are going to have a difficult time working with our clients.

Once the applicant passes all of the assessments, we then do an in-depth phone interview. Looking at their assessment answers, we ask questions to determine whether they're a good fit for our agency, and for our clients. Following the phone interview, the candidate will be invited to a face-to-face interview, where we spend time getting to know that candidate both personally and professionally. We'd like to know what they're looking for in a job so we can match them with a family whose needs will be a good fit. Next we will have them complete some training modules at home to give them a higher level of training that we require. After successful completion of the training we will check three professional references and two personal references to assure that they have the proper child care experience. We also run a national background check, covering all states. This includes checks for criminal records and the sexual offender registry. We match the candidate's experience with our client's needs. For example if the experience were only with school-age children, we wouldn't match the candidate with a client needing care for an infant. After the checks are completed and the candidate appears to be a good fit for one of our clients, we will have then interview with our client.

Details of caregivers' verifiable work experience also helps us appropriately place them for our back-up/temporary and corporate services. We qualify them for certain age groups where they have the experience, and when our client is booking a caregiver, only caregivers we have qualified for the assignment will show up as available to the client.

It's critical for us to be able to properly serve our corporate and family client base for back-up and temporary care services, so we have a large staff and are always bringing in new applicants to make sure we are properly staffed to handle the peak needs. Many of our caregivers are full time with guaranteed hours. We select additional caregivers for these services based on their qualification and experience as well as their availability to be on call and their understanding that this will not necessarily be a full time job. Most of them have been nannies for individual families. We keep track of trends and staff to meet our peak capacity needs—in fact we have never not been able to fill a job in our Charlotte market. In an ongoing effort to maintain the highest level of service, we require our caregivers to complete a certain amount of education during each year to stay within our system.

We consider job satisfaction of the nannies to be an important outcome of our work. Our nannies have been very satisfied with the families they have been placed with because of our thorough screening and matching process. Our back-up and temporary services allow nannies and other caregivers opportunities, and job needs when they are not currently interested in a full time nanny position or while they are looking for a full time position with an individual family.

How to Select a Nanny Agency

Selecting a person to care for children is one of the most important decisions a family can make. Therefore, if they are going to be working with an agency to help find a nanny, they will want to make sure the agency will properly match them with the best nanny for their family.

The first consideration is the process the agency uses to screen candidates. Families shouldn't expect less than a comprehensive screening process that includes testing, thorough background checks, thorough past employer reference checks, and interviews. Criminal and sex offender registry background checks should be conducted nationwide, as it's possible the location history of the applicant may not be fully disclosed. Clients should be able to see written evidence of all of the screening documentation to verify its existence.

Affiliation with one or more of the professional nanny organizations, such as INA, the International Nanny Association, or APNA, the Association of Premier Nanny Agencies, is one indicator of a professional agency due to membership requirements. Another thing to look for is that the agency has professional liability insurance coverage. We also recommend asking how the agency will follow up to make sure the family and nanny relationship is going well and what happens if there is some conflict with the nanny in the future.

On the corporate side, most of the selection criteria for selecting a nanny agency apply. Most companies will want to make sure there is a training program for caregivers in place that requires periodic continuing education and that it is properly administered. The other key for corporations interested in a back-up care program is that the agency has adequate capacity to meet the needs of their employees.

About Dominique Rice

Dominique Rice founded Perfect Fit Placement Nanny Agency in 2012 after witnessing many families had nannies that did not meet their expectations and needs. In order for a nanny placement agency to pair a family with a nanny that not only meets but exceeds the family's needs it is important that an agency gets to know both the family and the nanny and alas Perfect Fit Placement was born. Dominique is passionate about professionalizing the nanny industry and believes all families deserve quality childcare. In her free time Dominique enjoys traveling, spending time with family and friends, and loves college basketball.

For more information about Dominique Rice and Perfect Fit Placement, visit https://www.pfpnanny.com.

Building a World Class Industrial Sealing Products Distribution Business
By Robert Aliota

Introduction

Robert Aliota lived in Milwaukee, Wisconsin until he went off to college at North Carolina State University in Raleigh. After graduating from N.C. State he moved to Charlotte and entered the corporate world. Shortly after moving to Charlotte he met and then married his wife, Susan. He worked in technology-based companies handling data processing and selling hardware and software solutions. After working as an employee for a number of years, Robert started thinking that he wanted to establish his own business; one problem was to decide what kind of business he wanted. Having come from a family with several entrepreneurs, it was not a far-fetched idea to start his own company.

Robert concluded that he wanted a business that catered to a wide range of industry segments, and also had a consumable, (residual) element to the business model. He came to the conclusion that an industrial sealing products distribution business met his criteria, and in 1995 he established Carolina Seal. What started out as a small business, operated out of his garage, has grown into a multi-million dollar business now housed in a 20,000 sq. ft. building in Charlotte. It's truly a family business as his wife, Susan, has also been involved in company operations. Today, Carolina Seal has customers, including Fortune top 50 companies, located throughout the United Sates and the Americas as well as in Asia. Its manufacturing partners are located in over 45 countries around the globe.

In this chapter Robert tells the story of his transition from employee to entrepreneur, building a sealing products distribution business with unique value-added capabilities.

From Employee to Entrepreneur

After college, my very first job was with ADP, Automatic Data Processing. This was truly a blessing to start my career at such a fantastic company. The people, the training, and the experience provided me a great foundation of good habits and disciplines that would help me throughout my career. After four or five years I was recruited into the computer networking industry, selling local area and wide area network systems, hardware, and software. After working hard at being an over quota producer for the next several years and regularly working 12-hour days, I started down the road of thinking that I wanted to be working for myself one day. I grew up in a family of entrepreneurs; so working for myself was not a completely foreign concept to me. I didn't know what type of business I wanted to pursue, but I started thinking about criteria that I wanted to establish in selecting an industry. I wanted to sell a product or service type that could be sold to a wide range of industries and customer types, not just based around a limited market segment. Second, I wanted to be involved in a business where there were residuals, or repeat business opportunities involved, so developing relationships, and generating repeat orders, would also be important. The third one was really a criteria that would be in place once the business was up and going. My objective was to not allow any single customer to account for more than 12% of our gross sales. I never wanted to feel like I had too many eggs in one basket from that perspective. This was easier said than done, but was a good benchmark to have, nonetheless.

When I was vacationing with my wife, sister, and brother-in-law, back in 1994, I began discussing possible business opportunities and ideas I had. I realized that my brother-in-law's business in the Midwest met the first two criteria that I was looking for in my own business. He had an industrial sealing products distribution business that had many of the key business characteristics I was wanting to include in my business. After further conversation, we realized a lot of his manufacturing partners could use a distributor in the Southeast, so I took the plunge and incorporated Carolina Seal in 1995. At the time, my wife, Susan, had a successful career in corporate sales, so this allowed us to keep an income flow going, while I focused on getting our business off the ground.

Carolina Seal is an engineered products and solutions company specializing in a wide range of rubber, metal, plastic, and foam components for industrial applications. The parts supplied by the company are generally not the most expensive components in any overall assembly, but they are frequently some of the most critical sub-components that can lead to down-time in expensive equipment, product recalls, or warranty claims if they do not perform as intended. Typically our components are used anywhere there are moving parts in a manufacturing process.

Carolina Seal's business model can be broken down into two different "segments" within the business model. The origin of the business would be considered the "GI", or General Industrial side of the business. This side supports OEM, (Original Equipment Manufacturers), where the parts purchased go into an overall end product assembly. Examples of these types of customers include manufacturers of ATV vehicles, lawn and garden equipment, gear boxes that may turn the luggage belt at major airports, scuba-diving equipment, pump, valve or compressor manufacturers, and many others. The other, smaller, dimension of this side of the business is considered "MRO," or Maintenance, Repair & Operations. This part of the business supplies repair/maintenance parts typically used in the equipment or machines used to produce a final product. This may include parts that may help excavating or construction equipment run, conveyor systems, bottling equipment, or a wide and diverse range of other applications.

The other segment of this diversified business model includes an entire operation dedicated to the Chemical Transportation industry. This side of the business caters its "Best Practices" approach to safety and compliance for some of the largest chemical shippers in North America. This aspect of the business model started around 2005 and has been a rapidly growing segment of the overall business since that time. Many of the Quality Control standards Carolina Seal has introduced to this particular segment are now being embraced as the de-facto standards for industry.

As the business started to achieve a break-even nearly three years into the garage operation, we decided that Susan should leave her corporate job and take care of our first son. Not long after that, the unfortunate events of 9/11 occurred, and like most manufacturing and distribution businesses in the United States, we struggled for a while as the economy was suffering. Fortunately, with the skills and experiences acquired from her corporate jobs, Susan was able to step into the business, and make valuable contributions when and where needed over the years.

Around 2006, with a growing need for more office and warehouse space, as well as increasingly larger rent payments being required, it became apparent to us that it might make good financial sense to invest in our own building to operate our business in. We settled on a well-maintained 20,000 square foot office and distribution facility, located in Southwest Charlotte, and still operate the business from this location today.

As a "garage start-up" business, we initially lacked the credibility and resources to attract major accounts. Early on, we relied mostly on smaller "mom and pop" type operations, but as we continued to grow, and we increased our own level of knowledge, experience and resources, we gradually were able to bring larger and larger customers on board. Today, we are proud to support not only those same "mom and pop" operations, but also some of the largest Fortune 50 businesses in the U.S.A. We now ship parts to 48 states in the U.S., 13 locations across Canada, 7 locations across Mexico, and even a customer or two in Asia.

Building a Business with Unique Value-Added Capabilities for Customers

At the very beginning, a critical decision had to be made regarding what type of business model we wanted to build. Would we sell anything and everything and compete on price, or would we focus our time, energy, and resources on building a business that delivered engineering solutions and solved technical challenges. Today, we focus on what we do best so our customers can focus on what they do best.

Today, we not only have on-staff engineering support for our customers, but we also have learned the benefits of maximizing the niche expertise available through our manufacturing partners. We are aligned closely with some of the top, world-class manufacturers from all over the globe that each bring unique skills and experiences to us. This is how we are able to, collectively, deliver our customers the optimal solutions for their specific applications.

Each customer is unique and each product application can certainly be different, but the common thread imbedded among all of them are the best practices and principles required to deliver positive results. Operating with high-integrity, ethics, trustworthiness and for the well-being of our customers are just a few of the values we have embraced from the beginning. With respect to the engineering aspects of a project, we evaluate what type of material is involved, what manufacturing process is needed, (molded, machined, extruded, stamped, die-cut, etc.), what tolerances must be met, what certifications required, and perhaps when and how many parts are needed. All of these things, among others, are taken into consideration as we determine which manufacturing partner best fits the profile to help us deliver successful results to our customers.

One of the common challenges with the rubber/elastomeric industry is that some suppliers operate with more integrity than others. Since many of the parts are "black rubber," it is nearly impossible to the human eye to determine if the part produced is made with the agreed upon "pedigree," high-quality ingredients that will lead to longevity and strong performance, or is the part made with inferior ingredients to reduce the overall cost of production and greater profit margins for the supplier and/or the manufacturer. Both types of parts will look the same, feel the same, fit in the application the same, and even perform the same initially. Only after a period of time will the inferior part start to fail, prematurely, and potentially cost the customer warranty claims, product recalls, or even hazardous safety issues. One of the value-add services Carolina Seal offers is chemical and mechanical material analysis, based on the specific parameters of our customer's application. We help our customers identify the optimal material needed to maximize performance and results. Through a series of engineering questions and analysis, we help customers hone in on specific "material formulations" that will deliver consistent and repeatable results.

One of the more unique, advantageous benefits Carolina Seal also has is their own in-house Quality Control Lab. With this lab, we are able to perform in-depth material analysis on incoming products to ensure they meet ours, and our customers' high standards. We call this service, "MVP" service, Material Verification Protection. With our sophisticated lab equipment, we essentially take a "DNA" analysis of the rubber, which then is converted to a graphical format, to compare our approved batch of material to each subsequent shipment. This allows us to ensure our customers that they will get the same consistent pedigree material, each and every shipment. This certainly requires a bit more time, and cost, to follow this stringent process, but we have found the benefits, and peace of mind this offers our customers, to be more than worth the effort.

One of the challenges with the MRO segment of the business is that much of the manufacturing machines used in the U.S are made overseas, most often in Germany or Japan. One challenge for those customers working here in the United States is to find the replacement parts to help repair those pieces of equipment. The fact that we work internationally, and we have global manufacturing partners, we not only can supply standard U.S. dimensioned parts, but we also can obtain metric and custom sizes. We work with our customers to identify long lead-time replacement parts for custom equipment and then put custom stock in place to offer immediate availability. To take it a step further, another value-add service we offer is assembling a wide range of repair parts into "kits" so all needed repair parts are organized into one convenient bag. All individual parts within each kit are bagged, tagged, labeled and numbered for easy identification and ease of use. That's essentially another way that we create a significant value for our customers.

Case Studies

I have listed below a few brief case studies to demonstrate how we have helped manufacturers overcome quality issues with their products or assembly.

<u>Lawn & Garden Equipment</u>

Lawn and garden equipment is used outdoors and is subject to outdoor elements, such as sunlight, high temperatures, ozone, UV rays, and dust. A commercial equipment manufacturer was experiencing a high rate of failure with a custom molded rubber component that kept cracking and failing prematurely. The failure of the small part of expensive equipment caused field failures and warranty claims, causing unexpected high expenses and harming their reputation. The manufacturer asked us to get involved in developing a solution.

We had our engineering team analyze the application, functionality, and the exposure the part was subject to and discovered that exposure to ozone/UV light was the culprit. The manufacturer had initially specified the part to be made from a standard off-the-shelf material, but, as is very common, was made with inferior ingredients. Working with one of our manufacturing partners, we custom formulated a rubber compound for the part that was much more ozone resistant that fit their application better than the standard material that had been specified. The improved part has been in place for many years now, and the equipment manufacturer has not had any quality problems with the component since we went through the process and changed the material.

A typical obstacle in this type of situation is the investment the manufacturer has already made in tooling for the molded part. In this case they had already paid for initial investments of custom molds to produce their parts. Due to the change of component supplier, new tooling was required. The good news in this case was that even with the quality problems solved and the loss of investment in the original tooling, we were able to supply a part that was higher quality, and a lower cost, which offset their additional investment in tooling.

Overhead Doors

A manufacturer of commercial overhead doors used in a variety of industrial and commercial facilities experienced a variety of issues with a hinge used on the doors. The doors were typically used in applications that required the doors to go up and down quickly and repetitively during every day use. The hinge was made from high-density polyethylene material that was machined in-house at the door producer.

One of the problems they faced was the significant amount of space in their facility that was required for machining the door hinges in their facility. The company had limited space and they had to invest in large quantities of raw material to produce the hinges. Sophisticated CNC machines were required to machine the hinges and the costly equipment was expensive and difficult to maintain. Machining the high-density polyethylene also requires a lot of expertise and quality problems sometimes occurred during the manufacturing process. Due to the design of the hinge itself, the quality and performance problems occurred in the field with frequent complaints from their customers that the hinges were not adequately durable and were breaking or breaking off the doors themselves.

A number of years ago, the door manufacturer called us in to offer assistance in solving the many technical issues with the hinges. We conducted an engineering review to better understand the ultimate function of that door hinge, the part that was in question. In conjunction with one of our manufacturing partners we re-engineered the design of that part to offer much greater strength and durability. The solution was to mold the hinge into one congruent piece, and that completely eliminated the need for the company to produce the hinges in-house. This resulted in not only saving the space in their factory to machine the part, but we also eliminated the costly raw materials that were kept on hand and the time and labor for the in-house machining process. The end result is that we deliver them completed hinges, pre-labeled in bags of 50, immediately ready for installation. We even had their company initials molded directly onto the part itself, for branding purposes. Since the completion of our work on this project many years ago, the quality issues have been completely solved and no further customer complaints have been logged. The "re-engineering" of this part has been a huge success for our customer.

All-Terrain Vehicles (ATV)

A manufacturer of All-Terrain Vehicles frequently experienced a quality problem during their assembly process. This related to the fact that the product required 12 different sized black o-rings that performed critical oil or grease sealing functions in the product. All 12 of the o-rings were technically different in size, but ever so close to one another with the naked eye. Due to them all being "black and round," it was extremely difficult to tell them apart from one another. In addition, because these small, round, black o-rings were being installed into a black plastic assembly, you could hardly tell if the o-ring was even installed, or if it was missing all together.

After hearing about this challenge from one of their engineers, we knew we had a solution to this problem. We suggested "color coding" each of the 12 different size o-rings with a unique color to help differentiate them from one another. In addition to this benefit, we were now able to clearly see when the (now) colored o-ring was properly installed into the application. To this very day, we pre-bag these colored o-rings, in bags of 25, to make it user-friendly for their production line, and have not had a single issue since. This solution was implemented over 10 years ago and this has been the standard used ever since!

About Robert Aliota

Robert Aliota is the President and CEO of Carolina Seal, Inc., located in Charlotte, North Carolina. He founded the company in 1995, initially working from his garage. Carolina Seal has grown from humble beginnings, initially focused on small customers in the Southeastern states, into a leading engineered products and solutions company with customers throughout the United States, Canada, Mexico and overseas. Among their customers are a number of Fortune 50 global companies.

As this is being written, recognizing the unique capabilities of Carolina Seal, the company has been acquired by Sweden-based Trelleborg, one of the world's largest seal manufacturing companies. Trelleborg is a $3.5 billion world leader in engineered polymer solutions that seal, damp, and protect critical applications in demanding environments. Located in over 50 countries around the world, their innovative engineered solutions accelerate performance for our customers in a sustainable way.

Robert Aliota received a BA degree in Business Management from North Carolina State University and worked in data processing and computer hardware and software industries before founding Carolina Seal and focusing on the engineered products industry. The company was featured in the February/March 2009 issue of BusinessWeek's Small Biz Magazine and also in the June 2011 issue of Business Digest, a Paris-based publication.

Carolina Seal participates in a number of local and national charitable organizations, including Wounded Warriors, The Housing Authority of Charlotte and have supported many youth sports teams over the years, as well. They have also been proud supporters of South Mecklenburg High School soccer, where both of their boys played in high school.

Helping Small and Midsize Businesses Succeed Through Technology
By Steve Olp

Introduction

Steve Olp has over 30 years' experience in a variety of different businesses and industries. He was always on the user side of IT, but usually one of the people deeply involved with the IT projects during implementation. While with BP he moved formally into an IT leadership role, helping to rebuild the business systems for their Texas City refinery. Following that assignment, he then led the creation and implementation of multiple business and data systems necessary to support the remediation activities in response to the Deepwater Horizon oil spill in the Gulf of Mexico. He returned to North Carolina after retiring from BP with an eye towards applying what he had learned in large organizations to help businesses in the Southeast grow and prosper. He acquired TEAM Technology in 2014 and has grown the company organically and through acquisition to provide a variety of IT solutions for small to midsized businesses as well as some large multi-national companies.

In this chapter, Steve elaborates on typical challenges companies face with IT and information management, how to plan for IT projects, and highlights some case studies of successful implementations.

From Working Within Corporations to Helping a Variety of Business Succeed Through Effective Information Management

Working on the operations side in the corporate world, I learned a lot about the power of information technology (IT) and how much more effective organizations can be when information <u>and</u> technology are properly managed and implemented. I also observed the more recent growth of cloud computing and it's associated benefits of world-class security and cost effectiveness, even for smaller businesses. Having worked at BP for almost a decade and being involved in some very large scale business systems project implementations - first for the Texas City refinery and then for the remediation activities in response to the tragic Deepwater Horizon oil spill in the Gulf of Mexico, I gained a great deal of experience in matching the right technology solutions with organizational needs.

I returned to North Carolina after leaving BP with an interest in taking what I had learned and using that experience to help small to midsized businesses, particularly in the southeast region, better utilize IT tools to accelerate their growth and profitability. I acquired TEAM Technology, a small company founded in 1997 that had been primarily focused on IT staffing and enterprise resource planning

(ERP), in 2014. It provided the foundational platform to offer a wider set of IT solutions especially focused on small and midsized businesses.

TEAM Technology serves clients (small, midsized, and large) predominantly in manufacturing, distribution, and professional services industries. For smaller operations, we help individual professionals like one-person insurance and accounting firms. At the other end of the spectrum, we provide services to large and enterprise-sized clients – including a $2 billion per year manufacturer. For that client we support operations in the United States, Canada, and Latin America. Most of our clients are in the Southeast; yet we also provide services and support to clients in the Northeast and Midwest.

We help companies improve collection, interpretation, and management of their data; enable and enhance collaboration and communication among employees and with customers; and enable employees to work remotely and from mobile devices to post and access information, regardless of where they are working.

As a Certified Microsoft® Partner, we support the full range of Microsoft software and technology solutions. These include the Office365 product suite, Enterprise Resource Planning (ERP) and Customer Relationship Management (CRM) solutions, Document and Data Management – including cloud-based infrastructure architecture, Employee Collaboration, and other solutions.

We are a "one-stop" shop for IT solutions. That means we have the expertise and the experience to bring all the parts and pieces together in a holistic fashion for any type of technology issue, challenge or opportunity. Our goal is to help the small and midsize businesses that haven't had access to the professional IT resources we're able to provide at a manageable and cost effective price. This creates a competitive advantage for our clients, allowing them to grow faster and become more profitable.

Common Challenges for Businesses

<u>Data Collection and Analysis</u>

Collection and getting insight from data is a key strategic challenge for most businesses, whether they are a small one-person professional business, a midsized business, or a large international corporation. While organizations may be collecting a lot of discrete pieces of data, data by itself is not useful until it viewed in the proper context in which it then becomes *information*. With the amount of data literally exploding, we often observe businesses having a difficult time organizing and managing their data in a way that is useful in managing and operating their enterprise.

Many companies have staff spread geographically and there has been increasing emphasis on allowing employees to work remotely. With employees working in different locations, the ability to communicate and participate in process workflow can be challenging. Effective workflow management can become a strategic advantage, but in it's absence there's a liability.

IT Staffing and Resources

Small businesses typically have minimal internal IT resources, often just a small part of someone's primary job responsibility. Often, we see a variety of different ad-hoc pieces of technology that are being used to get the job done. Lacking a dedicated resource and/or IT strategy, there may be several opportunities being missed to be more productive through better management of data or workflow. Some companies continue doing things the way they have been for years and have not considered modern IT solutions; they don't realize the potential positive impact in capabilities and cost reduction that can be achieved by modernizing with newer technologies. Even larger companies with dedicated staff frequently need additional technology resources to develop and implement projects and bring them to a conclusion in a timely and cost-effective manner.

Data and Information Security

Security and infrastructure cost is a common concern. "The Cloud" is a relatively new concept: with this approach data is stored off-site and accessed through the public or a private internet connection. A common misconception is that having someone else manage key IT resources, such as in the cloud, will cost more than handling everything in-house. This isn't necessarily the case.

There's also a perception that the cloud is not as secure as having the hardware on premise, when in fact, the exact opposite is generally true. For example, for one of the cloud products that we support, the company spends over a billion dollars a year to keep that particular platform safe and secure. In contrast, any company that's not investing appropriately and devoting resources to secure their enterprise cannot ensure their data is safe and secure.

Maintaining Pace with New Technology

New technologies have exploded in the last 5 years. Keeping up with not just the technology but how to use it to remain competitive is critical. Many small and medium size businesses continue operating as they have for years, not realizing the potential to improve overall business effectiveness and capabilities, reduce cost, improve reliability, reduce downtime and scale their business. Companies that have an effective technology strategy have proven to be better positioned for growth and success.

Why So Many IT Projects Fail to Deliver Expected Results

There is an abundance of stories that may be found regarding the high failure rate of IT projects. These range from complete failure where the project was abandoned, to projects that were completed but failed to deliver expected results. Most of these failures began from the onset due to a flawed definition of the problem and the project requirements. As an example, business owners will think, "What I need is a new financial accounting package," so they'll go out on the Internet and search for financial accounting packages. Then, they'll look through the elaborate marketing information and find something that grabs their interest, then their problem becomes, they don't have that accounting package. However, they may not have thoroughly evaluated their actual business requirements and objectives. Although an accounting package may be a need, there are a lot of aspects that come into play in the differences between packages and offerings. Lack of understanding or definition of the true problem on the front end is one of the major factors that drives IT project failures.

New system implementations are complex projects with significant execution risk. Lacking a detailed plan covering all aspects required for completion is another frequent cause of failure. Without a plan, surprises can occur, and those usually end up with unanticipated extra cost, or additional time and resources required for completion.

Planning for Project Success

Identification of the real problem and developing a comprehensive implementation plan are critical for achieving a good outcome from any project, especially for any IT project. In an ideal situation, we work with the business owner and other stakeholders to discover the current challenges and opportunities for the business. The first part of the process is to identify and make sure that the problem to be solved has been adequately defined. Clarity on the business strategy is critical to understanding the problem as there needs to be alignment between a business strategy and a technology strategy. As an example, some companies are eager to expand and they may have technology limitations that are constraining their ability to grow. On the other hand, some sole-practitioner professionals may have more of a lifestyle business and they may not want to dramatically grow their revenue; they may just want to be more efficient with use of their time.

After understanding the root problems we are able to help identify the right manner to address those issues with the wide variety of tools available. While identifying alternative solutions, review of the business processes is another important and value-added part of the discovery. We often observe processes that are not best practices, so there's not much sense in taking a bad business process and migrating it to a new software platform. In such a case a business might as well just stay on the existing platform. During this phase, we challenge our clients to consider the best practices working at other companies.

The key objective in our client engagements is to help ensure clients achieve the maximum value from the investment in technology projects.

We utilize Microsoft's Sure Step methodology, modified with approaches we have learned while walking in the shoes of clients on the operations side of implementation projects. We document a very detailed project plan that is used throughout project delivery. The project plan communicates to the business owner and all stakeholders the purpose of the project, timing, planned outcomes and what to expect during project delivery. The plan also identifies all the risks associated with the project and outlines contingency plans for the various risk elements.

Change is always part of a technology project, and many times the need to change is the actual reason for doing a project. Change management is another key to project success and needs to be included in the planning process. User adoption of a new tool or process is critical and requires frequent communication as well as end user introduction and training. It's also important for everyone involved to understand the reason for change and the business case that is driving the business decision and to make it personal for them individually. If these elements are not included in the delivery of a project, then the risk increases that that project will be viewed as a failure or that the users won't be onboard with the changes.

The first two steps at the front end of this approach might cost 20% to 25% of the total cost of a project and when a business gets to that point it's time for a pause to reevaluate the business case for making the investment. If the problem is properly defined and the value proposition is confirmed, it's generally an easy decision to proceed to completion. On the other hand, if those don't hold true, then the project can be altered or if appropriate, abandoned before too much money is spent.

If all the planning has been done up front, the project manager becomes more of a risk manager as the steps are already clearly established. In our experience, by understanding the risk factors businesses are prepared to prevent those risks from becoming an issue. With a well-detailed project plan, the speed of delivery goes up, the cost of delivery goes down and the success of the project is remarkably higher because you don't have the pain associated with delays, extra costs, or surprises.

Case Studies

Client case studies provide examples of how businesses can increase competitiveness by implementing well thought-out IT solutions.

One company we have worked with is in the business of selling safety products that are for the personal protection of their customer's employees in the workplace. Typically, their customers subsidize the purchase of the products because employees are required to use the products in their work. This facet significantly increased the complexity of each individual sale transaction. Our client sells their products via their own retail stores, online sales, and on trucks that periodically visit their customer's manufacturing and distribution facilities. Historically their trucks were frequently on the road for days at a time and the sales and inventory transactions were manually posted. Data was not processed into the business system until several days after the actual transactions occurred. Because all mobile transactions were handled manually, hand written tickets from the trucks were manually entered into the system a week later resulting in delays and increased risk of data entry errors.

This client, a family-owned business, wanted to grow substantially. However, without technology and mobile connectivity they were limited in their ability to expand with data updates lagging so far behind the actual transactions. They had technology challenges with mobile connectivity presenting a key technology challenge.

When the company engaged TEAM Technology several years ago, they were a small multimillion-dollar company. A new vision evolved to become a leader in the safety products field beyond their relatively limited geographic market. IT was a limiting factor in their ability to achieve the vision and to outperform their competitors.

When TEAM Technology was engaged to develop a platform for this client, we observed that the home-grown system was insufficient to handle the client's anticipated growth. We analyzed their requirements and determined that a package like Microsoft Dynamics NAV would satisfy about 80% of their needs right out-of-the-box, with some customization to achieve 100% of their requirements. It was one of the biggest investments they had ever made and essential to provide capabilities for the growth that they planned. Today they enter all remote transactions live with sales and inventory data being updated in real time.

Our client has continued to leverage their system through upgrades and enhancements allowing them to quickly react to marketplace changes, which they were unable to do with their legacy systems. They have since experienced exponential growth increasing the size of the business substantially, so much that they are now a national leader in the industry, operating with a more accurate, timely, and cost-effective system. They attribute their Microsoft Dynamics NAV solution as a cornerstone in enabling them to achieve such fantastic, successful growth.

We have another interesting project in the final stage of implementation for a manufacturer of custom machined parts. It's another family-owned business with a new generation moving into managing the business. The owner has been running the company for decades and is very skilled with programming the automatic machine tools that produce their custom products. Programming the machines is a significant effort requiring several hours every day, usually in the very early morning hours before work in the factory starts. The company had many "islands" of information without an integrated system where the data could be easily located and accessed. They had an older accounting system but critical engineering information was kept in spreadsheets, without centralization or integration with other data.

This is a small company with great potential for growth due to their manufacturing leadership. They were at a point where they could no longer manage and grow the business using spreadsheets and outdated software. We were engaged to assess the situation and recommend a solution to remove these barriers to growth.

Initially, they believed they required an updated accounting package and that their most pressing priority was a way to interface the bills of material with the automated machines, eliminating the need to manually program the machines. As we studied this company's needs we recognized that they were being limited not only by the tasks involved with programing their machine tools, but by their information management practices throughout the company. Again, we recommended implementing a modern ERP system, specifically Dynamics NAV, as the platform for all their information - financial as well as engineering. We began the implementation on the financial side and then moved to the engineering and other business data.

Inventory item numbers didn't even exist because everything was being done on spreadsheets. We advised on how to organize an item number system for the families of products and then established all of the bills of material in the formal system.

Now, not only are their financials being managed in a much more efficient way, the financial system is also is directly integrated with manufacturing. They have a better handle on being able to forecast demand and capacities to the machines. They're able to manage their workflows on the plant floor better, so they can get their products made and out the door to the customers faster and more efficiently.

The final phase of this project is focused on addressing the client's initial issue – programming the automated machines. We are now in the process of interfacing the ERP system with the product specifications to the manufacturing machines, thereby eliminating the need for the tedious manual programming. We're giving this company the ability to run everything from one integrated platform and eliminate the obstacles that were in the way of their desire to grow.

About Steve Olp

Steve Olp is a seasoned strategic leader in business and technology. He currently leads TEAM Technology in their activities to support business clients with technology, data, and information management needs.

Steve holds a Bachelor's degree in engineering from NC State, a Masters degree in Business from the University of Maryland, and a Masters Certificate in IT from the University of Houston.

Steve has more than 30 years of management experience in a variety of roles and industries that include building products, chemicals, pharmaceuticals, textiles, energy, and oil & gas. Steve has led technology activities in some very large IT organizations, with budgets in the $40 million to

$100 million range, as well as much smaller organizations where budgets were only in the thousands. With his broad business and technology background, he is uniquely capable of finding and matching the right technology to address specific business challenges.

For more information about Steve Olp and TEAM Technology, visit http://www.TeamT.com

www.ingramcontent.com/pod-product-compliance
Lightning Source LLC
Chambersburg PA
CBHW070241230526
45470CB00002B/468